Destination Cortez Island

A sailor's life along the BC coast

June Cameron

Heritage House
Fine Edge Productions

Copyright © 1999 June Cameron

CANADIAN CATALOGUING IN PUBLICATION DATA

Cameron, June, 1929-
Destination Cortez Island

Includes bibliographical references and index
ISBN 1-895811-68-6

1. Cameron, June, 1929-   . 2. Cortes Island (B.C.)—Biography
3. Boats and boating—Pacific Coast (B.C.) I. Title

FC3845.C67Z48 1998 971.1'203'092 C98-910807-1
F1089.C72C35 1998

LIBRARY OF CONGRESS CATALOGING-IN-PUBLICATION DATA

Cameron, June 1929-
   Destination Cortez Island : a sailor's life along the BC coast /
by June Cameron
       p.   cm.
   ISBN 0-938665-60-X (U.S.). — ISBN 1-895811-68-6 (Canada)
   1. Pacific Coast (B.C.)—Description and travel. 2. Cameron,
June, 1929-   . 3. Pacific Coast (B.C.)—Biography. 4. Boat
living— British Columbia—Pacific Coast. 5. Boats and boating—
British Columbia—Pacific Coast. I. Title

F1089.P2C36 1999
910'9164'33—dc21   98-32225
                                                  CIP

First edition 1999

Heritage House wishes to acknowledge the financial support of the Government of Canada through the Book Publishing Industry Development Program, the British Columbia Arts Council, the B.C. Ministry of Small Business, Tourism and Culture, Canada Council, and the British Columbia Archives and Records Service for aid and assistance in our publishing activities.

Cover and book design: Darlene Nickull
Editing: Audrey McClellan

HERITAGE HOUSE PUBLISHING COMPANY LTD.
Unit #8 – 17921 55th Ave., Surrey, B.C. V3S 6C4

FINE EDGE PRODUCTIONS LTD.
Route 2, N. Valley View Dr., Bishop, CA 93514

Printed in Canada

DEDICATION

To all the pioneers who shared their stories with me. Especially Anna and 'Tad" Middleton, Dunc Robertson, and Irv Reedel who could wait no longer. We treasure their memories.

CONTENTS

-

ACKNOWLEDGEMENTS

When my children were young and I presented them with stew for supper, the invariable comment was "You cleaned the fridge today, mom," for the stew consisted of things new and old, some half forgotten in the back corners of the storage area, some from precious jars of condiments, and some newly bought for the occasion. Whatever the sources, the results were always consumed with gusto. This book is a kind of stew with sources new and old. Some bits came forward from forgotten corners of my mind, but most came from the memories of my relatives and friends, who greeted the idea with happy enthusiasm.

My father, in his 80s, before strokes robbed him of the ability to read and write, prepared for me four tapes of his life in the early days around Cortez Island. Listening to him talk to me seven years after his death was a lonely experience. These tapes and the family picture album formed the stock for the stew. Alice (Hayes) Merx, the last living member of my mother's family, contributed her girlhood memories. Friends such as Etta and Clarence Byers filled my ears with stories and sent me off gathering tidbits from long-forgotten old-timers. My best pal on Cortez, Nellie Jeffery, was an ever-present ingredient-checker as she has lived most of her 80 years on the island.

People like George Bone of Powell River supplied reference books from his private library, as did Helen Anderson of the same town. She also provided her memories of Turner Bay and hilarious jokes to lighten my load. My cousin, Rod Griffin, answered queries with twelve-page letters about his growing up at Blind Creek (Cortes Bay). When I needed fresh supplies for my boat I went to Refuge Cove, where Doris Hope provided meat for the local stew and a further helping of humour to carry with me on my rounds. The other people who helped with the cooking are all mentioned in the book. And since quality control is imperative, I owe a debt of gratitude to my editor, Audrey McClellan, for sniffing, tasting, and giving a final stir to the mix.

INTRODUCTION

An introduction really has to be written after a book is finished, for the thing evolves almost of itself until you reach the final period. I had no notion that, among other things, my memories of the coast would invariably include old apple trees, but there they are, in every chapter. I am not alone in noticing the apples, for other people who have explored the coast of British Columbia and written a book about it invariably comment on the traces they find of settlers who left little evidence of their presence beyond a few straggly fruit trees.

In almost every corner of the world one finds similar evidence of earlier civilizations. Perhaps this is a fortunate thing, otherwise what would archaeologists have to do with their time? Each wave of settlement left traces of its passage, whether they were the simple stone tools of a primitive tribe, the barrows of a later group, the stone buildings that seem to abide forever, or a few apple trees among the evergreens. These remnants are like surf on the beaches of time.

The first to arrive anywhere in the world must have sent word back to tell their friends about the marvellous soil, game, fish, trees, or gold, depending on what persuaded men of that age to uproot family and venture into new territory. To the British Columbia coast, besides those with useful skills to offer, came entrepreneurs who glimpsed opportunities for personal gain, creators of the ultimate in grandiose schemes: to build railroads to impossible ports with anticipated riches for those insiders who "knew" where to buy up land. To make these dreams a reality they needed hordes of everyday people to create a demand for supplies.

The advertising required to lure those looking for their golden opportunity showed up on billboards, in newspapers, and even in pulpits in Europe and the eastern townships, for with the spread of populations went the saving of souls. The intended quarry was the land-hungry immigrant who was unable to own property in the Old World and dreamt of the opportunity to till his own soil. They may not have comprehended the awesome space and distances between settlements in the sunset portion of the New World. But many heard the call and came.

My maternal grandfather listened and believed. He brought his gentlewoman wife and nine children to Cortez Island in 1917 with the dream of founding his own orchard, flower garden, and nursery; of exporting newly developed strains that he hoped to propagate; and of making a living from the fruit that he produced. He came right at the end of the golden first era, before refrigeration on coastal steamers, when it was possible to earn a bit of money supplying local industry with food. Grandpa Hayes was not alone. Traces of orchards litter the coast.

Farming was the industry that attracted the most settlers and it created more poverty than all the others combined. Certainly those fruit trees that remain on old abandoned farm sites have a right to bring tears to our eyes, for it proved impossible to supply the promised support system of transportation. Those who spotted the problem while they still had some cash beat a hasty retreat. The rest stayed on in genteel poverty or joined the men and women in other resource industries.

Anyone who endeavours to write a history, be it national or familial, needs to gather facts. This involves interviews where possible, and reading letters and diaries written long ago. I have tried to talk to two or more people about any given event, and like historians before me I find that history is in the eye of the beholder. I have done the best I can to take the neutral path when my raconteurs varied in their reports.

One thing I have done is leave out the juicy parts where they would bring injury to the descendants of those involved. I cannot tell you which husband and father spent weekends away in his boat with bottle and broad, so to speak. Nor can I tell you who returned from the war minus the family jewels, only to have his wife present him with another child a few years hence. Like Thomas Wolfe, I am certain that you can't go home again if you disclose the skeletons that exist in your own territory. To be unable to return to the land of my childhood summers would break my heart.

Although I started out to discover my own roots, I consider myself fortunate to have learned along the way about women of fortitude and courage. For every one who retreated to the city at the first sign of personal discomfort there were five who rose above the difficulty to become literally superwomen. If lack of vaccination robbed them of children, they had more; if adversity pressed them to learn to run a boat or start up a business on their own, they did. In a time when women did not have the vote and were not thought to have the intelligence to use it if they did have it, these people triumphed. There were also those who persevered in spite of matrimonial difficulties because they put the needs of their children first.

How I wish that I had asked questions as a youngster and recorded the answers. But here I am, at 65 years of age, delving into the microcosm of history on the British Columbia coast as experienced by my people, with much of the information already lost to time. With these restrictions in mind, here is the story of a few old-timers from the area of Cortez Island and Desolation Sound—the pioneers who planted the fruit trees you find here and there—and inseparable from it, the story of the MV *Loumar* and the many other boats and engines that were essential to the pioneers, for the ocean was their highway.

In his *British Columbia Coast Names 1592-1906*, Captain John Walbran states that Cortes Island and the nearby Hernando Island were named by Spanish explorers Galiano and Valdes in honour of Hernando Cortes, conquerer of Mexico. While that spelling has survived on most Canadian Hydrographic Service Charts, many of the pioneers anglicized the name and referred to the tranquil island west of Desolation Sound as Cortez.

Blind Creek was an early name for Cortes Bay, site of the Griffin family homestead. When other old-time names are used, the current name is given in parentheses at the first occurrence.

Unless otherwise identified, photos are from the Griffin/ Hayes family collection.

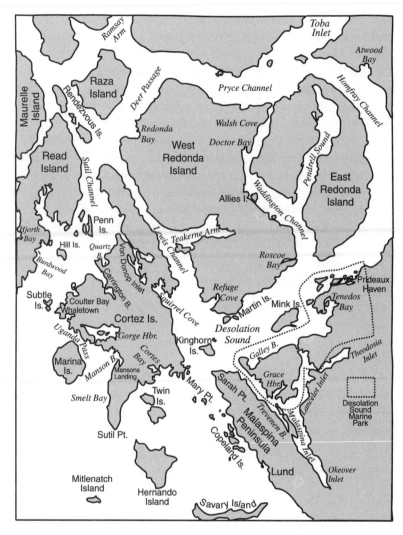

For June summertime during the 1930s and early 1940s meant a sea journey northwest from the Vancouver moorage, along the Sunshine Coast to Blind Creek and Cortez Island.

THE GOOD SHIP *LOUMAR*

Finding the old family album was what did it. I had not thought of the *Loumar* for years, but there she was in all her dark, shining beauty—36 feet of sturdy wooden boat, all gumwood sheathed and practical. Bought in 1930 for the sum of $750 at Coal Harbour in Vancouver, she was summer home to our family for nineteen years. In her we travelled up the B.C. coast to Cortez Island to spend the happy months of our vacations, and since five of my mother's married siblings and her parents still lived there, the *Loumar* also acted as transport for all kinds of occasions. But best of all she was our home, filled with apple boxes full of books from the Vancouver Public Library and most of the supplies we needed except the soft cakes of yeast Mother used for bread making. These we bought every other week at Refuge Cove.

Travelling on the *Loumar* allowed my brother, George, and me to pack each summer full of adventures. When my father, George Griffin, wasn't wielding the monkey wrenches that kept the motor going, he was reading or writing books. My mother, Marjorie, was always busy because she felt obliged to do everything it took to keep the household going, be it the floating home or the house in the city. If we children had any chores to do, being on the boat made them fun. In retrospect, probably the same held true for my mother, as all the pictures show her smiling.

The second year we had the *Loumar* it was moored in False Creek at Harold Clay's wharf, which was located where you now find fibreglass boats alongside the causeway serving as access to Granville Island. In the early 1930s Harold, a sign painter by profession, saw the need for mooring outside the Coal Harbour area. I think my dad must have been one of his first customers. The floats of Harold's marina snaked their way around the edge of the bank, made up of decaying sawdust and discarded lumber, that kept Rat Portage sawmill from sinking into the mud. The mill's log booms were located where an expensive

Marjorie and George Griffin proudly balance on Loumar's *foredeck in 1931, their first full summer of cruising.*

condominium now sits. How different are the condo's limpid reflecting pools from the oil-stained, smelly water that surrounded our boats. In those days, low tide in warm spring weather made you regret that you had to breathe to survive. Not only that, but the area was known as Rat Portage for a reason; of rats there were plenty, some as large as small cats.

Granville Island was a veritable seething mass of industrial action with huge foundries, machine shops, wire rope manufacturers, and a cement-making plant (the latter still exists today because of an astute long-term lease arrangement). The noise, smoke, and debris were awesome, and the leaching of oils and filth into the waterways was appalling. Next to the sawmill, in the direction of Burrard Bridge, there was a cluster of floathouses with squatters existing amongst the noise and flotsam. Fortunately for us, Sundays brought a lull in the activity, though the tugs bringing log booms to the inner creek came at whatever time weather and their schedule allowed.

The boats that shared the water with the *Loumar* were an artist's delight. Harold Clay's *Arrawac* was all neat varnish and white trim with a turquoise hull. One boat that especially fascinated me as a young child was not unlike the *Caprice* in which the Blanchet family cruised, except it had a toilet room on the back deck amidships against the aft wall of the cabin. I remember leaving my small donation within, but because I could not figure out the pumping mechanism, there it sat. I do hope the owner's children, who no doubt were chastised for failing to flush, have forgiven me.

The term "live-aboard" was unknown in those days; you just did it. Among those who made the dock a permanent home was a man called Rudy Kipling, who was a writer and was related to Rudyard, his famous India-born namesake. There was another local resident in the tough years of the Depression when unemployment insurance meant working at anything to which you could turn your hand. This old fellow lived in a cave just above the high-water mark, in among the discarded lumber, sawdust, and mud on the bank at Rat Portage. He used a stained piece of canvas as a partial wall to keep the wind and rain under some control, and he had a bed of sawdust and old clothes at the back. He cooked in the bottom half of a steel barrel and managed to survive by selling the crabs that he caught out in English Bay. All of Vancouver's sewers emptied into adjacent waters, so the crabs had reason to be there. Nobody, including himself, seemed concerned about his awful living conditions.

June and George Griffin on the back deck of the Loumar, *1931. As his knees suggest, George had been on the beach and found a "cradle" fish that he wanted to keep as a pet. He was refused. Note the rope tying June to the door latch.*

The tidal grid that served as haul-out for the boats was located just under the edge of the old Granville Street Bridge. One spring after completing the annual haul-out to clean and copper-paint the bottom of the boat, Dad dragged his weary bones home, had a hot bath, and fell into bed. While he was teaching the next day, Mother received an urgent phone call from Harold Clay: the *Loumar* had sunk at her berth! My mother sat down and cried; then the work began. I was too small to get involved in the excitement of the refloat, but I do remember marvelling at how the contents of a box of graham crackers had drifted to the ceiling, leaving soggy, oil-stained bits stuck everywhere. And I learned that you must always replace the bilge drainplug before launching your boat.

The *Loumar* had been built as a logging-camp tender during the heady days of the early 1920s, with no expense spared to make her a sound boat. The decks were smoothly planked and covered with canvas

No _____ Vancouver, B.C. _____July 9,_____ 19 32

Received from Mrs. Marjorie L. Griffin _____

____Two hundred and fifty ($250) ----------*Dollars*

In full payment for the hull known as the 'LOUMAR'

Length overall 35ft 9in, beam 9ft 6ins.

$ 250.00 _____ *mrs R upton*

The last of three annual payments that made the Loumar *ours.*

that was stretched on wet, then carried over the edges, with a capping strip screwed on to make a tidy, secure finish. When the cloth was dry it was painted, which gave you a few non-skid years before the layers built up to a slick finish. As was typical of the time, the walls of the cabin were tongue-and-groove three-inch cedar boards set on end. When a particularly dry spell of weather ended with rain, the huge curving timber that supported the after end of the foredeck would be decorated with a row of tobacco tins, suspended from nails over our bunks to catch the flood of fresh water. At that age I had particularly acute hearing, so I got to listen to the true music of the night as the tins filled at varying speeds. The drip into the ocean alongside added a percussion section. I revelled in the sound because I was cozy, warm, and well loved.

To keep the interior dry and to cook our food we had a large, wood-burning stove in the galley aft. Our job as children was to collect bark chips along the shore wherever we were anchored. This gave us an opportunity to explore the beach, as well as the challenge of getting out the myriad slivers that lodged in our fingers.

Bark was plentiful because all logs destined for the city mills were towed in booms. These were made up of floating logs penned between long boomsticks, with log "swifters" fastened across the top at regular intervals to hold the boom into a rectangular shape. Storms played havoc when the tows were caught in the open, and logs escaped. As a matter of course, when booms were in motion much of the bark was broken off and lay for the taking at the high-tide mark on beaches. It was full of salt, so it played hob with the chimney when we burned it in the stove, but it was free and easy to find. We kept it stored in gunny sacks under the back deck.

The Loumar *prepares to leave False Creek with cousin Roddy and June on the top deck and Marjorie at the wheel. You can see the houses in the West End and Burrard Bridge in the background.*

When all the spring repainting was finished, and when school was finally out for the year, we loaded the boat with what seemed impossible mountains of supplies. When we were at Blind Creek, shopping was restricted to the settlements at Campbell River, Squirrel Cove, or Refuge Cove, with Campbell River having little more to offer than Refuge. At the River there was a long dock threading precariously out into the fast water, and the Willows Hotel was the largest structure in a town that relied mostly on supplies arriving by steamship. It is no wonder our boat had to be well stocked.

The box I dreaded the most contained canned milk, which was the only preserved milk available at the time. We loathed it. Mother tried serving it hot, diluted with water and sweetened with sugar, which made it even more nauseating. The going theory (probably true) was that chocolate was bad for you on a daily basis, but I could have managed the canned milk in cocoa.

The box I most liked seeing was the one containing bully beef from Brazil. This was priced at two tins for 25 cents and was a staple for many coastal people. Even today it appeals to me. Our upcoast diet relied heavily on fish and corned beef, as there was certainly little fresh meat available. Vegetarian habits were just beginning to arrive on the West Coast with returnees from the British Army Corps of India, but the rest of us felt horribly deprived if we didn't have meat on the table.

We had to load enough flour to meet Mother's baking and bread-making needs. This was stored in large, gold-coloured, metal lard tins that could be picked up free of charge at bakeries, so they were readily available to the pioneers. During the worst of the Depression we could take one of these tubs to Jersey Farms Dairy on Broadway and for ten cents get it filled with skim milk, which was poured down the drains in the spring when the cows were fresh and overproducing on the farms. These metal containers with snug-fitting lids kept the damp out of the flour stored on board and slowed down the progress of weevils.

As you can imagine, all this stowage took time and patience, a thing somewhat lacking in my father. So while Mother finished the job, Dad took the car home and returned via the streetcar that conveniently deposited him at the south end of the Granville Bridge. Next morning we were on our way.

Most years the departure from Clay's wharf was fairly straightforward. We threaded our way past the other boats and pointed the bow toward the railway trestle that stood just east of the Burrard Bridge. This wood and metal structure carried the trams that ran from Steveston, at the mouth of the Fraser River, all the way to downtown Vancouver. When the *Loumar* wanted to leave port she waited, as had hundreds of boats before her, for the swingspan to open. Sometimes the operator was not in the booth but had to hurry the length of the bridge to open the tracks. When our turn came we eased through the narrow opening and headed for the fuel barge that was moored outside the Burrard Bridge.

One year when I was quite small we had an aunt and new baby on board, making the trip back upcoast to an anxiously waiting daddy. Just as we got well out into English Bay the engine turned cantankerous and all was shut down as my father got busy with the usual monkey wrenches. I could tell that things weren't going well by the stream of creative language issuing up from the engine room. Swearing in front of ladies was not done, so to relieve his stress he had invented a lexicon of polite expletives. Many "Sainted Michaels" and "Holy Peters" floated up and blew away. We children tended to cringe when this happened because the tone of voice was so fierce.

After an interminable length of time the boat suddenly began to lurch and rock as though the almighty hand of God were admonishing my father. Then we heard the bellow of a bullhorn. It was coming from the bridge of one of the Princess boats that was going around the *Loumar* in tight circles, with people lined up along the railing watching us.

When we finally focussed on what was being said we heard, "Are you in distress?" That seemed a ridiculous question under the circumstances. Pots and kettles were flying, the baby was screaming, and most of us were terrified. My dad responded manfully with a "No," to which the skipper replied, "Then get those distress flags down!"

Mother scrambled to retrieve the baby diapers from the rigging. She had managed to squeeze in a small washing while Dad struggled and swore. Just then the engine coughed and purred and we were off, with another lesson learned by a chastened crew about the marine signalling system. Of course Father blustered that he had known it all along, and Mother made her usual string of apologies.

Over the years the *Loumar* had several car engines, each one bringing with it problems for Dad to wrestle with down in the engine room. The most successful installation by far came from a sporty car called a Willys-Knight. The special feature of this power plant was something known as sleeve valves. This engine was both smooth and quiet, pushing the heavy weight of the *Loumar* along at a respectable eight knots. As most 36-foot hulls made seven at the time, this was a bit of a record.

To keep the engine temperature down, Dad carried fresh-water pipes out through the hull and fastened them along the starboard side of the keel. The hot water that would normally go through radiator pipes now used the ocean as a coolant. If anything went wrong it was usually in the distributor or the carburetor, not in the actual combustion process, although I do remember Dad cutting a gasket out of a piece of stock in order to seal a leak while we bobbled about at sea. He usually had me hold the flashlight for him, allowing me to observe engines close at hand at an early age so they were not an entire mystery when I eventually was running my own.

My memories of the *Loumar* cover that era commonly known as the Great Depression as well as the war years, when our coastal location brought a new set of rules. During the later years of World War II, when Japan and the United States joined in the fray, gun emplacements surrounded Vancouver and blackouts were common practice. If you wanted to drive your car after dark, the headlights had to be taped, leaving a narrow slit at the bottom for the light to shine through. The military had ultimate control over coastal shipping and sent out regular patrols of boats in what was called the Gumboot Navy. These former seine boats and substantial cruisers monitored all traffic coming and going around what were considered strategic sites. Leaving port in any vessel required adherence to strict regulations.

Once we decided on our day of departure, Dad had to go downtown to fill out all the necessary forms, probably in triplicate. He had to give our destination, the number of people that would be aboard, and the purpose of the trip. We had to have identity numbers both on the cabin sides and displayed in large letters on the top deck of the boat. The ones on top were to facilitate identification by aircraft patrols, for heaven only knows what dreadful harm a small cruiser loaded with children and bully beef could do. I do not have one of the official forms for the *Loumar*, but I do have one issued to Fraser Gavin's father for his fishboat. Because the fishing fleet was numerous, there was a special office for them at the fish dock in the main harbour. But whether you were a work boat or pleasure craft, you had to abide by the rules.

On the declared departure day you were required to leave, regardless of weather conditions. No doubt the expensive barometer had been rapped senseless by the skipper before he ever went downtown to fill in the forms. One year the inevitable happened—a strong northwesterly gale blew in overnight. Dad agonized about whether he should go downtown, cap in hand, to ask permission to delay the trip. He came back to the boat after a prolonged phone call to announce grimly that we were leaving.

Sometimes a run out of the harbour and around Point Atkinson in heavy weather is no more of a challenge than bucking into a sea anywhere would be. Other times, when there are big tidal changes, it can be a horror. Point Atkinson is at the junction of two major waterways. Howe Sound to the northeast is a large fjord that stretches back inland for many miles. The inner harbour of Vancouver leads to another long inlet called Indian Arm. A large change of tide in these areas needs enough water to raise or lower the surface of the sea by up to sixteen feet. When this water leaves on an outgoing current, the two flows meet off the lighthouse station at Point Atkinson, creating tide rips. If this junction is also lashed by a northwest wind, the ocean is churned into waves that meet in sharp peaks, then fall away and drop your boat into a deep hole. The watchful lighthouse keeper has saved lives when unwary boaters get caught in this turbulence.

It was into conditions like this that my apprehensive father pointed the bow of the *Loumar*. He planned to stay well clear of the point to avoid the worst of the slop. However, the patrol boat, with what must have been a sadistic skipper on board, was stationed near the lighthouse. It was our duty to seek out this vessel and wait while our identity numbers were matched up with the numbers of the boats on his list for

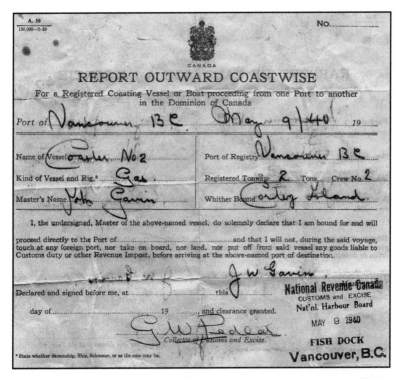

You did not travel the coast without the required paperwork in 1940.
Note the official spelling of Cortez Island.

the day. Instead of him coming out clear of the turmoil to meet us, we had to draw close to the point. All this would have been bearable, as we had been caught out in storms before, but there was an added factor. A large log boom had broken up in the area during the night. Huge timbers reared up from behind cresting waves or lay hidden in troughs waiting for us. All this left my parents in a decidedly unpatriotic frame of mind as they broke out the brandy supply later in the safety of nearby Snug Cove.

During this same period my uncle, Dick Finnie, had been struggling to get into Prince Rupert harbour in his troller in storm conditions when the patrol boat hailed him. Either not hearing the call or being too stubborn to turn back, he carried on, only to have a shot lobbed across his bows. The patrol boat captain was perfectly within his rights to have done so, and Dick was later billed for the cost of the shell. A few incidents like this made most skippers only too willing to obey the summons to heave to.

Like all small craft along the coast during World War II, the Jaitoon *had an identification number marked clearly on her sides and atop her wheelhouse. All marine activity was closely monitored to prevent Japanese infiltration from the sea.*

The stretch of water between Gibson's Landing and Welcome Pass was the most unprotected part of any voyage we made north. Since the *Loumar* had a long waterline, she was capable of making good speed, so trips up the coast were not too bad. Occasionally a northwester would get up while we were travelling on this part of our journey, so we would turn gratefully in to Secret Cove.

This beautiful, nearly landlocked harbour was almost empty except for the lonely government dock with the usual cream-coloured wharf shed. What set it apart from most ports was the tidy rock terrace stretching off to the south. The rockery was the work of a Norwegian World War I veteran, Fritjof Brynelsen, who had followed his brother to the area at the turn of the century and pre-empted the land where the dock was eventually built. He fished for a living but could not resist the urge to beautify his surroundings. The space behind the wall was filled with gravel and topped with soil that he had built up from seaweed, compost, and whatever buckets of earth he could scrounge from the surrounding territory. He created an Eden complete with roses and fruit trees. We children prayed for a storm in the fall so that we could visit him and enjoy his juicy pears. In time his nephews bought adjoining land, and one of them, John, built the original Jolly Roger Marina. The harbour is still a summer destination for various descendants who love it as I did.

June loved to visit Norwegian fisherman Fritjof Brynelsen,
seen here in 1940 on his porch at Secret Cove. His famous
roses grace the foreground.

One fall we had been given a chicken to cook on the way home. We were in Secret Cove because of a howling northwest gale and since it was my job to pluck the bird, I took it inside the wharf shed so that all the feathers wouldn't get lost. Frugal housewives kept them in those days to add to deflated pillows. I rolled the heavy door shut and worked in the sun-streaked gloom with its aroma of hay, wheat, and a bit of creosote mixed in. The walls had cracks here and there, so it wasn't entirely plucking by Braille, and I nearly had the job done when someone rumbled the door open. Feathers flew in swirls round and round, some blowing out the door to heaven knows where. No doubt it gave the steamship purser pause as he supervised the next unloading into that shed. Since I had already lost my precious hoard I finished the job by hanging the bird on the ramp railing where the light was better.

When I visited Secret Cove in the winter of 1994, the rock wall supported no aging fruit trees, just a driveway that skirted past the back of what appeared to be the old cabin, which is now a garage for a larger house. It seems a pity that all that fertile, hard-won soil has gone to waste. However, the nighttime stars shone as radiantly in this blessed spot as they did when I gazed up at them in those early years.

Most summers we worked our way straight to Pender Harbour and turned down the narrow passage that opens up on the right after we cleared the little islands, stopping to tie up to Harry Dusenbury's float. My dad had learned about Harry from my mother's father because Harry's brother was well known around Cortez Island. Often Dad needed something fixed, but other years we stopped here just for a visit, for the two men shared a common interest in making things work. The economy of the 1930s was the main reason my father returned to teaching school from a job with Pumps and Power, for he had been supremely happy using his brain and hands. With his creative ability for things mechanical he'd have been a great inventor.

There was a Mrs. Dusenbury, who brought a daughter and two sons into her second marriage. Together the Dusenburys had Iris, a real beauty of a teenager when I was young, and Roy, who looked like Harry must have done as a lad, handsome and dashing. When Iris was ready for high school we rarely saw Harry's wife again because she and Iris went to live in Vancouver. Given that Harry was strictly a man's man, with huge, shedding setters, fat cigars, and a fondness for the pub, one can easily understand her absence.

Harry had a floating machine shop when I was a youngster. He bought it in Vancouver and had it towed up and moored by what is now known as Dusenbury Island. At first he lived in a room at one end. With no engine or electric generator, every machine was manually operated. As in all blacksmith shops of that era, there was also a big forge. Since someone had to vigorously turn the handle on the bellows in order to make the fire roar, it is easy to see why Roy became a skilled mechanic at a young age. To operate his lathe, Harry pumped like fury on a treadle while he balanced on the other foot, guiding the cutting tool and frowning in the meagre light filtering through the dusty windows. The floor was made of oily planks that were littered with curls of metal, some still glinting silver as they came off the lathe. This was babbit from rebuilt bearings. I loved the way this word rolled around on my tongue. In fact the whole shop fascinated me.

We tied up at the Dusenbury's alongside their boat *Wabasso*. To get from our boat to the machine shop we had to walk on floats topped by uneven planks that were fastened on crossbraces between pairs of logs. These narrow floats were tied together with boom chains. Sometimes there were considerable gaps over which I had to jump. I vividly remember the sunny day that I lost my footing and plunged headfirst between two floats that were stretched apart by the current. I recall the sense of shock as my diaphragm hit the cold water, but after a few moments I became mesmerized by the utter beauty of the shafts of light

The Pender Harbour home of Harry Dusenbury still stands today. For many years a floating machine shop was tied up at water's edge to the right of the home.

shining through the gaps in the wharf. Gradually a feeling of euphoria took over. I woke up in my bunk some time later, absolutely furious that I was being kept in bed in broad daylight. One of Mr. Dusenbury's stepsons, Billy May, and his own son, Roy, had found my feet sticking up between the logs. If there were a chosen way to die, drowning would win for me. I lost my fear of dying at sea then and there. Also, I still enjoyed the challenge of getting to the machine shop to watch Mr. Dusenbury at work. And strangely enough, Harry himself drowned off the same float many years later.

I remember him as having knuckles the size of golf balls. Dad claimed this was from barehanded boxing in San Francisco where, as a young man, Harry had been a sparring partner to one of the big names in boxing. When I knew him his head was completely bald. Every so often when something puzzled him he would take off his black skullcap and run his big knobby hand over his dome as though to let a light shine in. He struggled along in his inadequate shop until the 1940s, when he acquired a proper machine shop with overhead line shaft and welding equipment from its site on the shore near Canoe Pass. The former owner had bought the shop unbeknownst to his wife and moved from Vancouver to Pender Harbour, expecting her to give up her teaching job in the city and follow him up the coast. This put such a strain on the marriage that he was forced to sell out, and Harry became the lucky buyer.

As the taut ropes suggest, Loumar *and* Wabasso *sometimes travelled tied together. Harry Dusenbury with his son Roy of Pender Harbour relax on the* Wabasso *while a smiling Marjorie Griffin steers the* Loumar.

In Pender Harbour Harry built a handsome brown house with a red roof and white trim. This could truly be called a house, not a cottage, because it was two-storeyed, and in the English way of thinking one did not live in a real house unless one had bedrooms upstairs. I learned from Bert MacKay, who grew up just down the bay from Dusenbury, that Harry had a scowload of lumber towed up from Vancouver and hired a Depression-starved carpenter at one dollar a day to construct the house.

There was also a sleek, raised-deck, cabinless cruiser that was built strictly for speed, with a narrow beam and huge nautical binnacle. Rumour was that Harry had used it as a rumrunner during the American Prohibition years. If so, his was not the only career launched during that folly. Certainly the *Wabasso*, as it was named, breathed stealth and speed with its very profile. He loved his boat and told me that *Wabasso* meant "little white rabbit."

Harry was a friend of John Antle, founder of the Anglican Church's Columbia Coast Mission. This mission provided vital medical and spiritual support to pioneers of B.C.'s central coast. John's big vessel, which carried his name, was often stored at Harry's dock, especially during the early 1930s when it was being eased out of service. Harry became involved in the push to have a mission hospital built at Pender Harbour. A local child with a ruptured appendix had been rushed out by boat to meet the city-bound Union Steamship, but the weather was too rough to make the transfer from small boat to steamship. The small vessel carried on to Vancouver under horrendous conditions. The child was dead upon arrival, and Harry vowed that no local person would ever again die from lack of medical help.

By 1932, when Marjorie stood on the John Antle's foredeck, the original figurehead of a naked woman had been deemed unsuitable by the Anglican diocese and was given to the Royal Vancouver Yacht Club.

The summer I was fourteen I left my appendix at the mission's St. Mary's Hospital in Pender Harbour. Had there not been a hospital I don't know what my parents would have done. I suppose we would have had to return to Vancouver, and as it was wartime we would have had the added pleasure of reporting to the patrol boat each way. But there was a hospital available, so I rowed with my mother over to it and was promptly put to bed. In those days you had to lie perfectly still for more than a week after surgery, which no doubt helped your adhesions set. My brother George revelled in coming over to see me so that he could tell me jokes and hear me moan with the pain of laughing.

St. Mary's Hospital had two small wards, one for men and one for women, plus a nursery. When women went in to have a baby they usually were kept there for up to two weeks. In light of today's practice of sending a new mother home almost the next day, this long stay seems excessive. But when you think of all the hard work a new mother faced in the typical pioneer setting, this was barely enough time for her to catch her breath. Many women said it was the only rest they ever got, and since their absence was anticipated, things at home were arranged so that the family could cope without them.

St. Mary's Hospital in Pender Harbour, 1930. The Columbia Mission boat is at the dock, which saw the arrival of many sick and injured patients. (BCARS E-07891)

The nurses were dedicated and kind, but as a child I never really got to talk to them as they seemed too adult for me to befriend. I found out years later from my friend Nellie Jeffery that one of the women was Nurse Brynelsen and was related to my kind pear donor. I learned from Bert MacKay that the Brynelsen family, which built the first beer parlour in Pender Harbour at Garden Bay, also donated the land on which the hospital was built.

While I was in hospital, George persuaded Mr. Dusenbury to sell him a little fishing troller called the *Wag* that was resting on a grid beside the machine shop. No doubt the boat came with a scaled-down price and a lot of help and equipment to make it functional. My brother would have been seventeen at the time and he was already well on his way to becoming a commercial fisherman. He had been catching fish and selling them to the fishing scow since he was eight years old. The day I was discharged he took me for a demonstration run in his new treasure. We went out at high tide through narrow Canoe Pass into Bargain Harbour and rounded Francis Point into the teeth of a nasty northwest slop. I vividly remember clinging to the mast and moaning "Oh! Oh!" as we lurched over each wave.

The *Wag* was a complete 24-foot salmon troller. It had poles, a fish box into which you put the gutted salmon, and an Easthope engine that sang a happy *kaputta-kaputta* song as it chugged along. There was a tiny wood- and coal-burning stove called a Little Cod, which was really only two small, round stove lids with an oval firebox below and a chimney above. There was a rectangular cleanout door low in the front so you could dispose of the ashes. It all stood on prettily curved cast-iron legs.

When George prepared the *Wag* for his second season of fishing, he converted the stove to burn coal oil by using one of the drip valves from an Easthope rocker arm lubrication system. This fed the stove with a steady drip of fuel. It was not a use the Easthope family had included in the engine's design and it was unpredictable and highly dangerous. This stove-feeding method was used by a number of fishermen at the time and resulted in a number of boat fires. If you got too busy fishing and neglected to watch it, the stove would flood with excess fuel, overflow, and light up your bilge. George must have been careful because the boat survived. He even resorted to burning coal oil in his engine if he ran out of fuel and the Easthope was still hot enough to accept the coarser fuel.

In later years I asked an old-time fisherman why all their boat names were so short. He replied, "Lady, if you gotta paint around all them letters every year you'd be dumb to pick a long word." So *Wag*'s name

When I look at the picture of Wag *with George at the tiller I can hear my musical brother singing "Wabash Cannonball" at the top of his lungs as he returned to Blind Creek after a day's fishing.*

The 36-foot Loumar *rests in Blind Creek with Grandpa Alf, Georgie, and George undertaking the annual task of copper-painting the hull.*

met the requirements and suited her nicely. She was certainly more of a puppy than a greyhound as she trailed along in *Loumar's* wake. I have a photo of her being towed behind the *Loumar* on a long line, so maybe there was still a lot for my brother to learn about the art of engine maintenance.

Most summers we made the run from Pender Harbour to Blind Creek in one day. However, if the winds were too blustery we went up Agamemnon Channel and down Jervis Inlet to a bay on Hardy Island. As we slipped into the quiet, the huge trees stretched out their arms to enfold us in their reflections, and Spanish moss hung from branches where kingfishers launched their dives. The owner of the island had not allowed any tree cutting or hunting, so this place had not felt the loggers' shears and the animals were so tame we could feed them by hand. A stream came down to the head of the bay where we anchored, and in the evening we could see the deer step ever so daintily up to the water's edge to get a drink.

I remember one summer when the weather became very hot the day we left Jervis Inlet. There were silky swells beneath the water surface but not a breath of air. George had always wanted to see what was at Stillwater, where the big surge tower stands, so Dad tied the boat to the outside of the log boom and we children rowed toward shore. It wasn't long before a fierce wind swept into the bay. It was all we could do to row back to the *Loumar* with me pushing on the oars from the back seat and George pulling. By the time we got to the boat the logs were leaping about so crazily that untying the lines was frightening, making us wish we were wearing logger's caulk boots with tiny spikes in the soles rather than smooth running shoes. We never did get near the tower, but I learned never to trust glassy, hot, windless days. I also learned much later that Stillwater was a complete company town with a store and everything, so we could have bought a much-longed-for ice cream had the weather permitted.

When George and cousin Rod pushed June down the Refuge Cove dock and stopped abruptly at the end, she almost slid through the gate into the salt chuck.

We seldom stopped at Powell River. There was a big company dock and the usual steamship landing with a small-craft dock to the south, but it was somewhat exposed to northwesterly winds. Also, if you had a white hull it soon became discoloured anywhere the waves splashed it with water, because the mill effluent that floated in a thick, grey fuzz on the surface was toxic. Locals who had to stop there soon learned that Lagoline Brand paint, which apparently did not have a lead base, was the only kind that was impervious to the stain. The first photo I have of *Loumar* shows her with a white hull, so my dad must have learned that lesson quickly.

Westview Harbour, slightly to the south, was not developed until after the war years, when the Union Steamships were booted out of Powell River to make room for the many scrapped warships that formed the new breakwater. When I was young we hurried past because by

In the summer of 1937, cousin Rod, George, and June were regular bowsprits as they anticipated their arrival at Blind Creek.

that stage of the journey we were all eager to arrive at Cortez, which we pronounced "cor-tease" and spelled with a z at the end.

Since we never got underway before Father had his usual unhurried breakfast, there was often a sharp afternoon northwest wind by the time we reached Savary Island. There was nothing to do but pound on. The *Loumar*, with her long hull and full, rounded bow, found these short, sharp waves distasteful. She rode longer waves more gracefully. George and I literally hung out the windows in our eagerness to arrive, calling out to each other as we recognized land masses and rocks. At long last the bow swung round the large bulk of Cod Rocks, we slid by Red Granite Bluff, angled carefully past the entrance rock, which was unmarked at the time, and nosed into the harbour. It seemed to us children that bells should ring and whistles toot. We were in Blind Creek at last!

THE HAYES CONNECTION

Our summer trips were excursions to visit my mother's parents, who came to Cortez Island in 1917, following the lure of advertising set out by the Anglican Church, the government, and the Union Steamship Company. The early ads spoke of 160 acres of free land that could be purchased for the cost of clearing it, putting in a garden, and building any kind of dwelling in which you lived at least six months. In five years it was yours. By the time Grandfather moved to the coast, the size of pre-emptions was down to 40 acres, partly because it was nearly impossible to clear the larger area of trees. The old measure of 160 acres reflected the usual allotment in the eastern townships or on the prairies, where clearing land was not such a challenge. On the coast, the acreage might include part of the ocean if that was what it took to complete the necessary shape.

Grandpa Alfred Hayes, from Watford, was a horticulturist trained at the London Polytechnic Institute. I still have his certificate. While arranging the floral displays at the Prince of Wales' residence he seems to have arranged something else as well because there was a "shotgun" wedding with a young lady in residence by the name of Bessie May. As the saying goes, "she married below her station" and in due time the couple was sent off to make a new start in Canada. The young wife died in childbirth on the voyage, leaving Grandpa a widower at the tender age of nineteen. He returned most of the trappings her family sent with them for establishing a decent household, but somehow the barrel containing twelve place settings plus serving pieces of heavy, blue-on-white bone china was overlooked. This china was later used for Sunday dinners, and numerous Hayes descendants have treasured pieces of the set on which the gold still sparkles and the indigo pattern seeps right through to the back of the dishes.

When Grandpa arrived in Canada in the early 1890s the country was still developing. Vancouver was in its infancy. In fact, the area south of False Creek was just stumps. Grandpa went to Winnipeg and was soon employed by the city, laying out the plantings for parks and actually seeding a lawn instead of just cutting the rough country grass. My mother said he was responsible for the choice of shrubs and trees down the centre islands on Broadway when Winnipeg began laying out those grand avenues that still make it a city of beauty. Not long after his arrival, Alfred and his brother Frederick, along with Fred's wife, began a light opera group so that they could continue sing-

Alfred Hayes and Florence Ashford on their wedding day in Winnipeg, 1899.

ing the wonderful music they had enjoyed in England.

Grandma Florence Ashford was the daughter of a country squire who raised carriage horses in Buxton, Sussex. Her mother died when Florence was four, so the little girl was raised by her older sister, Mary, with the help of the servants. After Mary married and moved to Winnipeg, her younger sister joined her. Through family connections, Florence was employed as lady's companion to the wife of Sir Hugh John Macdonald (son of Sir John A.) when he was appointed lieutenant-governor of Manitoba. The new lieutenant-governor had a lot of official travelling to do, and because ladies simply did not travel unaccompanied by another female in those days, Florence went on a number of tours, not the least of which included the official opening of Lake Louise Hotel.

When the new lieutenant-governor's residence was built, Grandpa Hayes was employed to lay out the gardens. I do not know if my grandparents met among the flowers, at the light opera presentations, or at church. They were married in 1899. The babies began arriving within ten months with astonishing frequency. In the space of thirteen years she had nine, all born at home and many of them premature.

Mother told me of one childbirth session when she was awakened during the night by the sound of her mother crying out. Young Marjorie slept in an alcove off her parents' bedroom at that time. She heard the voice of the doctor as he arrived but was told to "just roll over and go back to sleep, dear, it's all right." To a small child it probably didn't sound all right at all. In the course of nine home deliveries, all undertaken with suitable Victorian decorum in which ladies exposed nothing, Grandma was so badly mangled that the marriage bed must have been a place of terror. Total exhaustion brought on menopause at 40, no doubt saving her life. By the time I knew her, she looked like a puff of wind would blow her to Hernando. I rarely saw her out of bed in later years.

Throughout the years of child rearing, the young couple could not afford any full-time help. When the nursemaid who came to help immediately after a birth was dismissed, Grandma was on her own, trying to cope with doing everything by hand as well as managing her growing brood. My mother said that each older girl got to take complete charge of one younger child. (Years later my Aunt Florence confessed that she used to sneak spoonfuls of the sweetened condensed milk that she was supposed to be mixing with water to put in the bottle for feeding my youngest aunt.) But childcare was as far as delegating chores went.

It's a pity *Cheaper by the Dozen* had not yet been written as Grandmother could have used some organizational skills. My mother said they were never allowed to do the dishes because Grandma was afraid of breakage. I still have a cookbook that was sent out from England to help Grandma with her household tasks. One chapter deals with cookery for the poor. The lady of the manor is further instructed on how to manage the help. I trust that Grandma used the book to prop open a window to cool her fevered brow, there being little other use for it.

Grandma and her growing brood spent the summers at Willow Point on Lake Winnipeg. I'm sure she was glad to get out of town so that she could lower her housekeeping standards. They lived in a big tent with a wooden floor. Given the sand and gumbo that Gimli is famous for, they certainly wouldn't pitch a tent right on the ground.

Grandpa spent weekdays in Winnipeg, but he kept a speedboat in the Red River, right below the house on Wardlow Avenue, for transportation to Lake Winnipeg. Maintaining and manoeuvring a boat

At Gimli, Manitoba (Willow Point), the Hayes youngsters—from left to right, Nerine, Bettie, Florence, Jack, Marjorie, Dorothy (in the rowboat), Art, and Nora—play in the lake, c. 1914.

up the Red and Assiniboine Rivers through lochs and storms no doubt served as preparation for life on the B.C. coast, where boats were the basic means of travel.

Nine children and persistent migraines left Grandma almost an invalid. The doctor recommended sea air (on reflection, a vasectomy would probably have done the trick), and one day at church Grandpa heard the Reverend John Antle speak about the wonderful opportunities that existed on Canada's West Coast. Obviously Reverend Antle could have sold anything, as he had single-handedly raised funds under the auspices of the Columbia Coast Mission to supply the coast with a ship that included both a doctor and a minister on staff. Over a period of time he established small hospitals at strategic coastal locations including Pender Harbour to serve the logging camps and many scattered settlements in remote corners of this convoluted area. He fervently believed that physical health was as important as spiritual well-being.

When Grandpa found an opportunity to speak to him, it turned out that the mission was desperately in need of an engineer for its ship, the *Columbia*. In those days, anyone who could keep an engine running was classed as an engineer, so Grandpa was hired. I suspect that Grandma was not consulted, or if she was, no one thought to mention the primitive offerings in the way of housing, roads, and higher education then available in the west. Certainly the move signalled the end of schooling for my mother, who was then sixteen.

As Grandpa was needed immediately, he set off, leaving my grandmother to solve the logistics of moving the family to the coast. She did not know that nice furniture was hard to find out west, nor did she know about the settlers' special on the trains. This special allowed you to load all your things into a boxcar while you literally camped out in a passenger car in basic surroundings, sharing a stove and single toilet with other travellers. Everyone carried their food, dishes, cooking pots, and soap in a wooden box so that travel expenses were minimal, and you could save enough with this cheap accommodation to afford the freight on larger items that you wanted to take along.

All the touring Grandmother had ever done was strictly first class, so for the move out west she sold the piano, the marble-topped sideboard, and all the rest of the solid walnut furniture from their nine-room house on Wardlow Avenue. She packed what clothing and linens she felt she could carry, plus small objects that she treasured. I have among my loved possessions a pair of Dresden figurines that made the trip along with a wicker hamper of German-made dolls. With these few inappropriate things the Hayes family left Winnipeg to set up housekeeping in the west.

In those days, downtown Vancouver consisted mostly of wooden buildings and open space. Many hotels had connecting doors between the rooms, with the toilet and bathrooms located at the end of the corridor, and it was to such a place that the Hayes came to wait for their upcoast trip. Their intended destination had been Quathiaski Cove on what was then called Valdes (now Quadra) Island. This was the location of the mission headquarters at that time and it made a lot of sense for the family to settle there if Grandpa was going to be working on the mission boat. At the last minute, however, they were asked to go to the area of Cortez Island called Clytosin, because the school there lacked the required number of pupils and would have to close if new students did not arrive. So they boarded the Union Steamship, meandered their way upcoast, and stepped off at Manson's Landing.

In 1917 the dock had a freight shed as it does today. There was also a small float and ramp so that local people could come in by boat to

After the Hayes family arrived on Cortez, the log school at Manson's Landing was assured a schoolteacher for years to come. With seven Hayes kids, almost half the students were from the new family on the island. Back row: Marjorie Hayes, Anna and Rose Manson, Miss Lettice, Nick Manson. Middle row: Art, Jack, and Florence Hayes, Wilena Smith, George Marquette, Veronica Tiber, Ethel Tiber, Bettie Hayes. Front row: Colin Thompson, Arthur and Marjorie Pickles, Helen Marquette, Bernadette Petznick, Dorothy and Nora Hayes.(Alice Merx photo)

pick up mail and passengers. On land there was a small waiting room to the left as you stepped onto the shore. Beside this was the original Manson trading post, a rectangular building made of sawn timbers with a door in the middle and windows on either side, looking not unlike the early Hudson's Bay Company forts. By the late 1910s the old store was run by the Farmer's Institute as a co-operative, a type of enterprise that some people think was invented just recently. The first Manson home, a cottage, was past it toward the end of the sandspit.

At their first sight of the landing, the smaller Hayes children began jumping up and down, saying, "Look at all the Christmas trees," although my mother remembered much of the interior of Cortez Island as a sorry sight to behold. The burning of logging slash the previous fall had resulted in a large fire that got out of control, blackening much of the land.

The Manson "Big House" near Manson's Landing included seven bedrooms and was later known as The Lodge. (Alice Merx photo)

My Aunt Bettie said that when the children cried because they missed their friends and school in Winnipeg, Grandma got them all singing to cheer them up. It wasn't long before they found new friends, as the island seemed to have many like themselves. Unlike the Hayes family, some had brought along their furniture.

Cortez Island attracted many people from England, Scotland, and the Shetland Islands. No doubt those from the latter came with the encouragement of the Manson brothers, who were from the Shetlands and who built their trading post at the Native settlement of Clytosin on the east coast of Cortez Island. Some came in response to glowing letters about the possibilities from not-yet-discouraged pioneers. The earliest settlers on the coast came around the Horn, at the southern tip of South America, bringing what they hoped would be adequate equipment. Some canny travellers from Europe shipped their goods the long way by water, but took advantage of the economy class in the train for themselves.

Before the turn of the century, Hernando Island near Cortez had a large settlement. The depression of the 1890s and the lack of a reliable market for their produce put these people so far in the red at the trading post at Clytosin that they gave their land to pay off their debt. This left the Manson brothers the owners of the whole, timber-loaded place. The gold strike at Bonanza Creek in the Yukon in 1896 drew some of these settlers north, likely to further disappointment. To the south of Cortez, Lund had many Swedish families among its first settlers. This clustering of people encouraged much social activity.

I'm sure the arrival of seven beautiful Hayes daughters on Cortez livened things up also, but like most settlers, Grandpa could have used a preponderance of sons. Early pictures show what I take to be boyfriends putting hand to axe, splitting froe, or what-have-you. (Those of us who feel the world was invented in our lifetime are surprised to see excellent black-and-white photography of that era.)

For a couple of years the Hayes family rented the furnished Manson house not far from the steamer landing. This fine-looking building boasting seven bedrooms, one of only three carpenter-built homes in the area, had been put up to house the large Michael Manson family. This family would have been even larger except that a diphtheria epidemic in the late 1800s took the lives of five of the first six children within a week, including a newborn infant. Michael's wife Jane came down with the disease while in hospital to have the baby, but she survived and had to go home to an almost empty house. The courageous and beautiful Mrs. Manson went on to produce another family, which included two sets of twins. I can't help wondering if the disastrous epidemic didn't also wipe out much of the Native population that had frequented the trading post at Clytosin.

By the time my grandparents came, the Big House, as it was called, was empty. The owners were living on Hernando Island where Mr. Manson supervised the logging. (I can remember as a small child seeing the long timber jetty built to carry the railway cars full of logs past the beach at Stag Bay on Hernando.) When the Hayes family rented the house there was a huge vegetable garden. Grandma said that people marvelled at the size of the vegetables she grew. Considering the shortage of water at the site, they said that it must be wonderful soil. In fact it was sandy and dried out quickly, so she got up early on dewy mornings and hoed in the moisture around each plant. Also, the children hauled seaweed and starfish up from the beach to supplement well-rotted vegetable scraps used for fertilizer. It appears that Grandma had finally managed to delegate some chores. Today you can find the remnants of the Big House garden in the few fruit trees at the picnic and rest stop just along the road from the dock at Manson's Landing.

My Aunt Alice remembers life at the Big House. She said that she was awakened one night by whooshing sounds that came from the direction of the ocean. When she called out in fright her father told her it was the blackfish (killer whales) breathing as they broke through the surface of the water. If they passed in daylight you could count up to twenty of them in a pod. They chased the salmon that schooled near the shallows. Alice also reminisced about the May 24 get-togethers held on the sandy beach at the lake. Henry Hague would bring his Victrola record player with tubular wax records so they all could sing along to songs like "Listen to the Mocking Bird" while they celebrated the Queen's birthday. At one such picnic, Mr. Hague bit into a wasp that had pre-empted his sandwich. In no time at all he was choking as his airway became constricted. Rose Manson quickly grasped his tongue, punctured it with a hatpin, and hauled it forward out of his mouth, thereby saving his life.

In later years the Manson house on Cortez became known as The Lodge. It formed the nucleus of a set of small rental cabins that fronted onto the sandy beach south of the steamer landing. If you search along the shore just into the edge of the woods you will find the level stretch where the cabins stood and a few ends of metal water pipe protruding from the bank. These cabins were still in use in the 1940s until the Union Steamships ceased to call at Manson's.

Any housewife unfortunate enough to live in the Big House had to cope with people dropping in for a visit and a cup of tea while waiting for the steamship to arrive. The boat stopped in twice weekly on the way upcoast and once on its way south. As the schedule depended entirely on the amount of freight being handled at the ports of call, one never knew precisely when the whistle blast would announce its arrival. Sometimes the wait extended over the meal hour, with the inevitable result. I can remember going to the Big House myself after a precarious ride on the back of Grandpa's Model T truck, which served as transport for anything from lumber to people. As we had my frail, gentle Grandma with us, we were all invited to stay to tea.

I have no doubt that the persistent crowd of tea drinkers was part of the reason that the Hayes sought other accommodation. Another reason was that by 1919 Grandpa had to quit his job on the *Columbia* because he couldn't conquer the persistent seasickness he experienced while down below with the engines in any sort of a sea. This brought an abrupt halt to the family's steady income.

The Hayes' next home was the big log house built by Ernie and William Bartholomew. The brothers were away working at logging camps, and Ernie was still a bachelor, so the house was unused and available. It still stands today under the name of Fairhaven, near a huge fir tree on the road to Blind Creek (Cortes Bay). More recent owners have built additions to the house and have further modified it by replacing with aluminum the four-foot cedar shakes that originally

Ernie Bartholomew with Bill Illman's Babe in front of Ernie's log house.

covered the roof. These were split from straight-grain virgin timber and would have lasted virtually forever but were hard to match when new wings were added to the building.

Ernie lived out his years there with his wife, Mabel Gertrude, who had come from England as a 40-year-old spinster in answer to a letter in a lonely-hearts column in the London newspaper. She actually had intended to marry someone else, but when she met the respondent she changed her mind. Mabel had been on the stage and continued to wear her white face powder and make-up until she died. Adding to her startling appearance were the tiny veins in her eyes, which became black over a period of time because she and Ernie put drops of silver nitrate in their eyes every day, thinking this would prevent blindness. She lived a fearful life on the frontier, keeping the doors locked at all times, although she went out for daily walks that often ended at her neighbour's for a cup of tea.

Apparently she had a small private income from England that gave them money on which to live. Ernie even employed a handyman who lived in a one-room shack on the property and was paid the enormous sum of five dollars a month for doing the outside work. Ernie needed the help because he did all the cooking, laundry, and dishes. It is pos-

*Nerine and Marjorie model the latest in gutta-percha
bathing hats during the summer of 1921 near Manson's Landing.*

sible this was a sort of pre-nuptial agreement. If that was the case, Mrs.
B. was one smart cookie. Yet by all reports they were a loving couple.
The road that runs past the house was named for Ernie Bartholomew, a
fitting tribute to a tiny, hardworking, humorous, kindly man.

It was while the Hayes family was living at the Bartholomew place
that my mother became close friends with John Manson's daughters,
Rose and Anna. By then my mother, Marjorie, was eighteen and Bettie,
her next younger sister, was sixteen and a half. The girls, especially
Bettie, had been begging to be allowed to go to the dances that were
held in the Big House. When Rose, who was then 21, said she'd be
responsible for them, Grandma gave in. She told them they had to be
home by midnight. The girls dutifully returned at the appointed time
but grumbled that they'd missed out on most of the fun because things
were just getting started by then. With many people having to travel a
great distance to get to the dance and, no doubt, with the loggers in the
crowd barely having had time for a nip of liquid courage, the dancing
didn't begin to get lively until the early morning hours. People stayed
until dawn anyway, so they could see to get home.

Grandma finally acquiesced and let them stay for the whole event,
with the condition that they had to be up to go to church with her in
the morning. She said that since she was going to be awake all night
worrying about them, they weren't going to be allowed any sleep either.
It must have been a drowsy bunch that filled the pews on Sunday.

My dad, George Griffin, came to the island in 1921. He was a Welshman, born in 1898 in the Roman fort town of Caerleon, and he went to school in nearby Newport where, true to the British system, he was already streamed into the naval architect program by the time he entered what we would call Grade 7. When he was thirteen, his parents decided to emigrate to Canada and settled in Edmonton. Young George's new school found that he was already proficient in calculus and blueprint-style art but could hardly write a coherent paragraph, so he had his work cut out for himself when he elected to become a schoolmaster. Upon graduating from the teacher-training program at the University of Edmonton, he found work in various rural settings before deciding to seek out warmer coastal weather. In Victoria that first summer he was joined by his young brother Joe. They shared a job as a waiter while also sharing their only white shirt—which necessitated some hasty washings and ironings between shifts. As fall neared, George answered an advertisement for the teaching job in the Manson's Landing one-room school and the die was cast.

Each settlement had its own school board at that time, and I believe my father told me that Cortez Island had four. In those days you needed eleven warm little bodies in order to open a school. The Hayes family nearly made up a sufficient number of pupils on its own. The Manson's Landing schoolteacher was boarded in rotation, first with one family and then another, and was charged $48 a month board. The amount of his monthly salary—$110—was shared equally between Victoria and the school district. I saw a list of teachers' names and their salaries that showed my father's right at the top of the scale, partly because of the level of his certificate. He was hired when the school board felt particularly flush with money, as there were many tax-paying families in the vicinity. A teacher's job description included all the cleaning of both the school and the two privies. He had to stoke the wood-burning heater, carry the drinking water from the well, and clean the windows, leading to a fair amount of chore delegation spread around among over-sized grade repeaters. Of course his responsibility also included lesson preparation and teaching up to ten grades.

It likely wasn't too long before the lonely young teacher sought out company at the Bartholomew house. Grandma must have been keenly embarrassed by the lack of decent furniture when the young teacher came to call. The house was a one-room cabin with a large wood-burning stove that had originally belonged in a logging camp kitchen. It looked the part, with its huge stovetop griddle and silver railing along the

This 1921 photo shows teacher George Griffin (left) with his sixteen students including five Hayes kids (Nora, Jack, Florence, and Dorothy in the back row with Alice mid-point in the front row). Photo donor Mike Herrewig stands far right. (Mike Herrewig photo)

front to protect the cook's belly. But I suppose cooking for eleven was hardly a small task. There were rough shelves along the back wall, with a table built of shiplap surrounded by chairs in a mixture of styles. For a bedroom the parents slept in a corner that was walled with strung up sheets. By this time Art was away working for Cougar Smith near Campbell River, and young Jack slept on a cot in the corner. The female children slept in the attic, which was accessed by a notched log propped against the outside of the front gable.

My favourite story from that time involved the big chamber pot kept upstairs for the youngsters to use during the night. Apparently it became full. Rather than make the cold wet trip down the slippery log and over to the outhouse, the last child to use it misjudged its capacity. Grandma was heard to say in her strong British upper-class accent, "Oh! I say, I say. This won't do," as the overflow trickled down through a crack in the ceiling and into the main room.

When it came the Hayes' turn to board the schoolteacher, Grandpa suggested that if George was willing to take potluck he could board for free in exchange for helping with the work, which was a smart offer to make to a broke but healthy young man. By this time Grandpa was commuting to Powell River to work on the company's townsite construction, so he needed an extra pair of hands around the house to keep the woodbox full. It wasn't long before Grandpa started talking about his plans to search for a suitable pre-emption site where he could begin raising fruit for sale, so the two men were soon off tramping through the brush, looking for the ideal spot.

One day, on a tip from John Manson, they slid down the bluff to the east of what would later become the Jeffery place and landed in a fine bit of alder bottom near Poison Bay (a name that stuck after John Manson set out poison bait there to catch the wolves and cougars that harassed his sheep. Grandfather promptly renamed it Ashford Bay, but modern charts show it only as an indentation opposite the north end of the Twin Islands). It included a natural meadow with a swampy area in the middle and a grove of young fir trees nearby that Dad said consisted of one- to two-inch stems growing so tightly together that you couldn't squeeze between them. A search of the district map, which was printed on oilcloth for durability, and which Margaret Schindler of Powell River still has a copy of, revealed that this was a 40-acre site that was available for settlement. The prospective settler's job was to locate the nearest corner post, which the surveyors had placed years earlier, and measure off the lot. Dad said this was a horrendous job involving hours of crashing around in the bush.

Now the work really began. With Grandpa's priorities well in place, the first job was to clear out a 50-by-50-foot garden space where vegetables were planted and where Grandpa heeled in young fruit trees that he had been gathering in anticipation of having his own plot of land. It was the girls' job to chop down and limb the multitude of fir saplings and make an eight-foot-high, deer-proof fence by forcing the peeled stems down into the soil close together, then weaving the branches among them for strength. This would serve to protect their plants until a house was finished and the entire pasture could be properly surrounded by the usual high picket fence made from split cedar that would last a goodly few years. In time, each tree had its own picket fence in case the deer penetrated the stockade.

With the garden well in hand, the next priority was the house. Dad said there was a fine straight fir tree standing right beside the chosen site, which was on the beginning of a rocky ledge just east of the garden. This magnificent evergreen was more than eight feet through at the butt, and the lower third was limbless, with the tree rising up to about 150 feet. Using falling axes and a long falling saw, and perching on springboards, Dad and Grandpa cut the tree well above the level of the butt and bucked it into four-foot lengths that they then split with wedges and a sledgehammer into what were called bolts. These long chunks of fir were so straight grained that they could be split into shakes as though they were cedar. The fir shakes were used on the walls of the house. In later years they aged to a beautiful burnt sienna colour. The stump from the old tree was still there, covered with ivy, when I last visited the site.

With the tree out of the way, the foundation was prepared, using flat stones and cedar posts cut off to make a level surface on which to place the three longitudinal supports, 32 feet in length, made of squared-off fir tree trunks. Cedar poles 28 feet in length and 6 inches thick were placed crosswise on top of these supports to serve as joists. Dad said that the poles were split lengthwise, one piece was turned, and they were placed double, heel to toe, to even out the thickness. An adze was then used to level the surface and make it ready for the sub-flooring. The sub-flooring was formed of four-foot shakes, thickly cut and stagger-seamed, then nailed with countersunk nails so that the surface could be smoothed with a shipwright's adze. Somebody must have been skilled with a sharpening stone. There was an upright circular one at the Hayes' place all through my childhood. You sat at it and pumped with your foot on a section of levered board, much like the system used to turn a potter's wheel.

The plates on which the wall was to rest were cut from fir logs that had been squared as much as possible. On these were set cedar poles for studs. These were cross-braced half way up and angle-braced at frequent intervals. On the outside were nailed the beautiful fir shakes prepared from the lovely old tree. The walls were capped with more fir logs cut down to size, and cedar poles were added for rafters.

Shingling the roof was a breeze after this because some of the young-sters had discovered a great many cedar shingle bolts washed up on the beaches. Apparently these were easily lost as they were often stored before shipping in open pens that were vulnerable to storms. Jim Spilsbury, who grew up on Savary Island, recently told me about los-ing a whole pen of bolts when he was a lad. His summer's work was washed down a dry streambed by a large squall of rain.

Dad said they scrounged stray cedar bolts from as far away as Reef (Sutil) Point. They used the rowboat that Grandpa built while they lived at the Big House, and although it was flat bottomed with cross planking and heavy as could be, it served the purpose admirably. The

George Griffin splits roofing shakes, with a froe ready on the bolt and a huge wooden club raised to strike a blow. These heavy clubs were fashioned from old knots that "pickled" on the beach below high water for many years until they hardened almost to steel.

shingles were split with a froe right at the beach. The children hauled the finished shakes up the hill as their contribution to house building.

All of this was accomplished by the fall, when Dad had to get to work at the school where he taught a class of twenty pupils in nine grades. His students included the younger Hayes children as well as many others. When I asked my dad how he coped with such a wide array of subject matter and so many children, he replied that as much as possible he involved the children in teaching each other. The noise, with so many teachers at work, was far above the level approved by the school inspector, so he taught the children how to behave when this august personage arrived.

The Hayes family lived on at the Bartholomew place for a while but moved into their unfinished new house before winter. The windows used to close up the walls came from Vancouver via the Union Steamship and were made of hand-laid glass. You could see the waves and dimples in them in the right light. There was some finished lumber used in the house, no doubt made at a local mill, but the pioneers were able to make most of the structure right out of the bush. By the time I remember it, there was a plate rack above the wooden wainscoting that held Grandma's precious wedding gifts of figurines and demitasse cups that we children beheld with awe. The floor in every room but the kitchen was carpeted with Powell River cloth, a heavy, creamy-white canvas about three-sixteenths of an inch thick. It was used at the mill in the paper-making process and every so often was available secondhand.

My Aunt Alice, the youngest of the Hayes children and still bright and well in 1998, remembers when they first moved into the house. The Byers brothers came to log the land around the site, partly to open it up and let more light into the garden spot and partly to give Grandpa a needed infusion of money. The logging skidway ran right past the corner of the house. One day the horses were struggling with a large log when one of them stepped in a hornet's nest that had hitherto escaped the activity. The horses heard the angry whine of the insects and charged away with the log as though it had been a matchstick.

For years the lower property, later developed by my Great-Uncle Arthur Ashford, had a pleasant view of the sea as a result of this logging and was kept quite park-like by the industrious herd of goats that kept all young trees under control. Grandpa always meant to build a substantial home on the rock outcropping where now stands a post-and-beam house put up by a more recent owner, a dentist from Lethbridge.

No sooner was the Hayes house built in the early 1920s than the community hall construction began. Money for the project had been raised over a period of years by a variety of means, not the least of which were dances held in the large combined dining room-sitting room of the big Manson house. Henry Byers and Wally Aldrich provided great music and there were gallons of tea and coffee with which to wash down the heaped plates of sandwiches and cakes eaten by the hungry settlers. In summertime the dances were held right at the wharf after the Union Steamship had left because everyone was there anyway. Among the musicians who improvised at the wharf was tiny Ernie Bartholomew with his mouth organ, which he always carried in his hip pocket.

Besides energetically attending dances, everyone who was able worked to prepare building materials. My dad worked with John Manson cutting shingles and hauling them up to the site with John's horse.

About this time, Dad's young brother Joe, who had followed George north and found work logging nearby at the Paukeneum camp, met and began courting my mother's next younger sister, Bettie. That would be a relationship that caused its own surprise. Since Dad was dating Marjorie, both young couples attended the opening dance in the new hall. Dad said that their enthusiasm for dancing took them to such places as the cookhouse at the Stag Bay logging camp. On one unforgettable trip to Campbell River, a southeast storm made the trip home an eye-opener after an all-night party.

Nerine, Grandma Hayes, Marjorie, and Florence in the back row,
Dorothy, Alice, and Nora in the front, with the handbuilt Hayes
homestead behind.

In one of his "get-rich-quick" schemes, Joe Griffin teamed up with a buddy named Bob Earl and bought a boat plus all the necessary equipment required for becoming handloggers. Apparently they were unable to get a licence, the deal fell through, and Grandpa Hayes got their boat for a few dollars. It was a 32-foot Columbia River hull with an 8-foot beam, powered by a Yale one-cylinder gas engine that had been built at the New Westminster Iron Works. A special feature of the boat was a leather universal joint in the shaft. This kind of flexible connection had been used in early automobiles, so its use in boats is not surprising. In the marine application there were two hollowed-out plates that were held apart by a thick pad of leather. Each plate had two bolts in opposite corners that went through the leather but not into the other plate. Large washers supported the heads of the bolts, so the leather pad became distorted as the shaft turned, but the bolts did not pull out. This allowed for misalignment and for the inevitable flexing of a wooden hull in sloppy weather. When Grandpa approached a dock he could slow the propeller by heaving on a lever that tightened an asbestos-lined metal band encircling the flywheel. If he wanted to go into reverse, however, he had to stop the engine by pressing down on a metal tab at the base of the spark plug, which shorted out as it hit the engine block. Then he restarted with the flywheel turning in the opposite direction. This resulted in some hair-raising dockings, to say the least.

The Columbia River hulls were flat bottomed, with the propeller and shaft angled down well aft. You could run the forward two-thirds of the boat onto rollers and pull it up on half-log tracks with the help of a hand winch. This arrangement fitted Grandpa's needs, as the bay was exposed to southeast gales.

By the time that I remember Grandpa's boat it was up on a rolling grid well above the high-tide mark in Ashford (Poison) Bay. But during its saltwater days this boat served the family well as they struggled to make a living on Cortez Island.

THE SEARCH FOR JOBS

In the early years of the twentieth century Powell River, about 30 miles down the coast from Cortez Island, became the site of a huge paper-making plant. The area was chosen for its plentiful supply of both raw materials and water. The paper mill grew beside a river system that was home to one of the largest sockeye runs in B.C. When a dam rose up to supply power and water to the mill, however, no fish ladder was built into it, so the salmon were unable to pass the barrier. In those days people thought little of the consequences of killing off a spawning area, as the seas were loaded with fish.

There was always work to be had by local people who supplied produce to the camp and provided the needed labour for the construction process. Not only was there a mill, but there was also a large, growing townsite that had to be built to house the mill employees and their families. My grandpa was able to take advantage of this bonanza because the boat he had acquired provided a means of travel and a place to live while he joined the work gang. Given the long hours workers put in in those days, it seems likely he stayed at Powell River until a project was finished, then took time off to attend to home chores. If the weather was bad during his visit home he left his vessel in Blind Creek, anchored just off where the government dock is today.

The job at Powell River provided a source of income that continued throughout the early 1920s and helped tide the family over until the fruit trees came into production, although the wages weren't high when you consider how many people he had to support. At that time a painter earned five dollars a day, but Grandpa, although a horticulturist, would have been hired as unskilled labour and likely earned less. His job was building the wooden sidewalks alongside the roadways in the town. Frank Tooker, who grew up on Cortez, remembered Grandpa working on the walkways that went from the hospital in Powell River to Church Corner, where there were three churches, and on past the firehall. Frank

Powell River as it appeared when Madge Patrick arrived from England as a five-year-old with her parents. (BCARS A-04190)

went to school in Powell River and caught rides to and from Blind Creek with my grandpa. To get home from there, Frank had to walk to Manson's Landing and then row up past Whaletown to his home at Coulter Bay as there was no road connecting the two ends of the island.

When the mill was first built, any visiting boats anchored right in front and passengers went ashore by dinghy. In time a rock breakwater was constructed to the south. This breakwater and the large log rafts anchored to the northwest provided shelter for the short dock. To get to town you had to walk a gravel road that curved up from the beach.

According to the records in the Powell River Museum, the house construction project began in 1911, when 21 houses were built. Prior to that, all the men except the officials lived in bunkhouses, but to attract and keep a stable population of mill workers there had to be accommodation for families. This building program continued steadily, and the mill had regular staff to supervise construction labour. Interestingly, the foreman was one Harry Middleton, a name that was later shared by the machinist at Squirrel Cove. When a huge mill expansion took place during the mid-1920s, 114 new homes were built over a period of two years.

The firm of Armstrong and Morrison undertook actual mill construction. It set up a camp of fifteen large tents, with seating for 400 workers in the dining room. This instant construction-workers city made up the largest such "temporary" accommodation in the province.

The townsite, neatly laid out in streets named for various trees, was bisected until 1920 by the logging railroad that carried huge loads of logs through the centre of town and on down to Michigan Avenue by the water. The old movie house that still existed in 1998 fronted right onto the track. One wonders how many pets were flattened on the rails.

Madge (Patrick) McGillivray, who still lives at Powell River, remembers arriving as a little girl on the steamship *Cassiar* in 1911 when the only way to get to the shore from the steamer landing was by walking on a two-plank-wide bouncing ramp. She remembers crying in fear every step of the way. Her father brought his wife and two small children from England, coming by steerage across the ocean with all its attendant crowding and constant seasickness, then crossing Canada on the settlers' special. In Vancouver he heard about the opportunities at the new mill, so continued up the B.C. coast. Because her father had come with his family, he was given one of the half dozen houses already built above the mill site. He came trained to do something called "back-tending," but as the mill was not yet operational he was handed a paintbrush. It didn't take him long to figure out that the painting trade would involve no shift work, so he elected to stay on at that job.

As the years went by he acquired a little gas boat and took his family on holidays away from the stench of the mill to the bight just north of Lang Bay. Today you find the name of Patrick on one of the roads leading to the shore of the bay, and members of the extended family still live above the sandy curve of beach.

Madge says that my grandfather would have had a choice of places to shop for food. The company store carried everything from boots to biscuits, but there was also, surprisingly enough, a store on the ground floor of China House. This was a bunkhouse for the many Chinese labourers who worked on railway construction and nearby logging shows. Sing Lee ran the store until the mid-1920s and sold mostly fresh produce and eggs along with rice and the usual Chinese cooking supplies. As well, once each week a farmer arrived in his boat with a load of seasonal produce. He piled it in a child's wagon, later a wheelbarrow, and pushed it up and down the lanes so that the housewives could come out and buy. Finally, it was possible to order groceries from Woodward's in Vancouver. The store shipped orders twice weekly on the Union Steamships, but you had to go to the dock to pick up your order, and the local officials made it plain that it was in your best interests to shop at the company store.

Powell River before scrap warships were sunk to form a breakwater.

Madge said that most of the labourers who worked on construction set up their tents all higgledy-piggledy in the large clearing on the south side of the mill. She said there was a large bathhouse with toilets and showers where they could get cleaned up. There was also a Chinese laundry down by the beach that would have been a godsend to the many bachelors working at the mill.

The house that the Patricks moved into had running water, but the toilet room was on the back porch, a not unheard-of location in those days. In fact, pictures of English cottages in London during World War II still showed toilet rooms "at the bottom of the garden," right where the outhouse once stood.

The hillsides surrounding Powell River were ugly. Junk wood was left standing, creating a mangy-dog effect. By the time I arrived, the greening had begun, but the area from Scotch Fir Point at the mouth of Jervis Inlet, all the way north past Powell River to the Sliammon Indian village, bristled with burned-out snags, the result of severe forest-fire damage. According to the *Powell River Digester*, the Powell River Company newsletter of the time, the amount of forest damaged by fires in British Columbia far outstripped the areas denuded by man. With so many small logging operations in progress and so many isolated settlers burning wood in their stoves, the chances for accidentally lit fires were enormous.

I well remember one night when I was small and we took the *Loumar* out into Baker Pass so that we could view the awesome fire raging on Vancouver Island from Campbell River down to Black Creek. But most of all I remember passing the settlement of Powell River by boat and marvelling that a company could own a whole town, especially one so neatly laid out with the large houses clustered together and the little ones in tidy rows behind.

Grandpa took time out from working at the Powell River townsite to build his own house before returning to the company project. Through all this coming and going he also persisted with his first love: fruit and flower cultivation. He bred new stock, corresponded regularly with Luther Burbank, the famous plant breeder and horticulturist in California, and kept meticulous records of weather and crop production. It was undoubtedly hard to hit the orchard big time living in such a remote place with no quick air service such as we have today for exchanging cuttings. Among the many new strains he developed were a Florence Ashford floribunda rose with a glorious perfume, and a yellow plum that was sweet right to the stone. This was a bonus as most of the early varieties of golden plums led you on with sweetness, then puckered up your mouth with the last few nibbles.

Lack of income and nine kids to clothe and feed must have taken their toll, but no matter how tough things were, the house was always surrounded by beautiful flowers. My cousin Frank Hayes said that the first fuchsia he ever saw grew there, hanging in all its abundant glory from the porch roof beam. And my christening photo shows us nearly dwarfed by climbing roses and Shasta daisies.

The Hayes family had developed methods to stretch a dollar by this time, many of them learned from other settlers. Mother said that the usual breakfast was porridge. One day they had it hot; the next day featured fried mush cooked in flavourful meat drippings, which formed an important part of the diet (pioneers worked too hard to store up any cholesterol). In fact, bread and dripping was a common lunchpail meal at the time. In the early years they kept an old cow to provide butter and milk, but at one point she became mired in a bog. When they finally found her and struggled her out of her mud prison with a block-and-tackle rigged from a tripod, she was too far gone to survive. The goats that replaced her provided odd-tasting butter because of their leafy diet, so dripping was a tasty alternative spread. My Aunt Alice remembers walking with the mail to old Mr. Hague's place on the lake near Manson's and revelling in the thick slices of homemade bread, butter, and treacle that he prepared for them. She says that it seemed to her as a child that she was always hungry.

The older girls found work wherever they could. For a while my mother walked to Paukeneum to work as cook's helper, called a flunky, while the oldest sister, Nerine, spent most of her time in Victoria where she was able to find work and lived with family friends by the name of Hughes. When my parents first met, Mother was dating a young sailor from Victoria by the name of Guy Hughes. From what I understand, when things began to look serious his mother put her foot down. She had other plans for her son. It was likely a good thing that he acquiesced so readily. My mother could have married him and the mother-in-law to boot.

Deep down in my heart I feel that Mother saw in the young schoolteacher a way to get off the island. By then she would have seen the toll pioneering took on young mothers. The lack of easy access to medical facilities and the dreary winters when all your time was taken up carrying firewood and drying laundry on a rack hung over the stove were enough to discourage the hardiest soul. Whatever the reason, she accepted George Griffin's proposal, smelly feet and all (we used to call him "Old Gorgonzola Foot"). By then he had a better-paying position lined up at Terrace, where he went off to work in the fall. In December 1924 he came down to Vancouver to catch the Union Steamship to Cortez, and the Reverend Alan Greene married them just after Christmas. In a box containing two unused lace handkerchiefs, a gift from my father, I found the list of wedding presents and donors. The gifts were all things to contribute to gracious living, likely ordered well ahead of time from the Spencer's or Woodward's catalogue and transported up from Vancouver on the steamship. There was no last-minute buying on the part of these pioneers.

Mother's honeymoon was the trip up north on one of Canadian Pacific's Princess line boats. Here she found out what was meant by cold weather. Dad said it was so cold that the sheets froze onto the metal bed frame at the foot of the bed. Yet pictures from that time show a lot of happiness. One of her sisters and her younger brother spent time in the school there and lived with them, setting a pattern for later on. And although they lived so far apart,

Shortly after their wedding, Marjorie and George Griffin wait in Prince Rupert for the train to Terrace and the beginning of a new life.

The 106-ton Columbia *was launched in 1910 and plied the coast for almost 50 years, bringing medical as well as spiritual aid to remote settlers. (Vancouver Public Library 38415)*

Mother remained close to her mother. They exchanged letters every week as long as my grandmother lived. That's a lot of writing when you realize that Grandma lived to her eighties. She also kept a diary through all the years of her life, as did Grandpa.

At the end of the summer of 1925, when my mother was six months pregnant with my brother, Grandpa decided to take Grandmother, my mother, my dad, young Alice, and her brother Jack to Vancouver on his boat to buy a replacement engine. It had been a dry August and the planking in the boat showed gaps at every seam above the waterline. They weren't ready to leave until late afternoon, so Dad assumed they'd go at first light, but Grandpa was used to the Coast Mission's schedules from when he worked on the *Columbia*. He announced that a moonlit, calm night was their best time for travelling, so off they went.

With the boat so heavily laden, the water began coming in the seams that would normally have been above sea level. Dad said he spent most of the hours of darkness working the lever on the bilge pump that was situated out on the back deck. Sleeping bodies covered the bunks and floor and all went reasonably serenely until they were off the mouth of Jervis Inlet. There Grandpa spotted a lantern being waved to and fro in the middle of the fairway. He veered over to see what was the matter, and a trio of somewhat inebriated loggers announced that they needed a tow. They had developed engine trouble and one of their group had methodically thrown each spark plug over the side as he determined it was not producing a spark. Needless to say, the toolbox contained no spares.

Grandpa towed the loggers to Irvine's Landing where they insisted that he accept three dollars worth of gas for his help, necessitating the waking up of a very disgruntled fuel-pump operator. The journey continued and late in the day they came into a large pod of California whales just off Gibson's Landing. Everyone was apprehensive but, as usual, the whales went about their business, ignoring the overloaded boat. Grandpa caught an ingoing tide at First Narrows and they were soon tied up at the foot of Denman Street, behind the arena that was Vancouver's only large home for travelling shows, whether wrestling or Yehudi Menuhin. Mother and Dad

Reverend Alan Greene became the director of the Columbia Coast Mission and regularly visited the coastal communities aboard the Columbia. (Vancouver School of Theology 5-1058)

caught the next boat to Prince Rupert; Grandma and Alice visited with the oldest daughter, Nerine, who was now working in Vancouver; while Grandpa and Jack worked on the boat.

After some scrounging around scrap yards, Grandpa found a Reo truck engine for $25 and set to work installing it. The engine bed had to be rebuilt, and when the new power plant was installed there was hardly any room left below, so in time he had to extend the cabin as well. To save money, Grandpa directed salt water right into the cooling system. He intended to install freshwater pipes along the keel when he was back at Ashford Bay, where he could use the haul-out grid for no charge.

Alice remembers that on the way home the engine quit in the night off the entrance to Pender Harbour. She, Jack, and Grandma used pikepoles to keep the boat off the rocks as it bumped its way up Agamemnon Channel in the dark while Grandpa muttered over the

Grandpa's boat at the wharf in Vancouver with relatives clustered on board and the arena in the background.

engine. A family of porpoises blew softly by in the dark, leaving a glittering trail of phosphorescence in their wake. At Cortez, recharging the battery remained a problem, so Grandpa constructed a windmill-driven generator down by the workshop at the beach in Ashford Bay.

Meanwhile, my brother duly arrived at the Prince Rupert hospital and spent his first six months in the teacherage at Terrace. It was in Rupert that Dad met someone from Pumps and Power, a company that supplied and serviced water pumps and, in later years, irrigation systems. When the Terrace school district added a high school and did not give him the principalship, he resigned and they moved to Vancouver. There he found work with P and P, installing pumps in the Fraser Valley. Dad's prize possession in those days was his newly painted Stern's Knight coupe. Later, when the company began appointing relatives of the owner to most positions where money was to be made, Dad decided to head for the Vancouver School Board office. He found work at Model School (now the City Square shopping centre), where one of his pupils was Jack Merx, who was later to marry my Aunt Alice. With a job well in hand, my parents moved into a house at Thirteenth and MacDonald Street in Vancouver.

The year Georgie was two, my mother not only had her sister Nora staying with them while she finished school, but she also made room for a boarder in an attempt to make ends meet. That summer Dad took his young son and headed upcoast on the steamship to help Grandpa

In 1928 times were good for George and Marjorie Griffin. Here, a year before June's arrival, Marjorie sits in their Stern's Knight roadster with young Georgie.

out with work around the farm. When it was time to get back to teaching, Grandpa elected to take my dad and Georgie home by boat. They travelled at night, and the usual round of bailing the bilges filled part of Dad's trip. By the time they reached Grief Point it was blowing up a bit from the southeast, but Grandpa pushed on. The engine began running hot, so Dad spent more time with the bilge water, this time ladling it over the head to try to keep the temperature under control. They pulled in to Dusenbury's at Pender Harbour and took the engine apart. There was salt water mixed with lube oil, no doubt the result of Grandpa's early cooling arrangements. They did what they could to rectify this problem, put things back together, and started out late the next day. Off the White Islets the engine quit and they could not get it started.

A tug was moving slowly past them in the dark with a log boom in tow, so they paddled mightily and managed to make a line fast to the boom, after which they fell onto the bunks in exhaustion. A wind got up during the night and finally their mooring line parted, leaving them adrift near Balfour Pass. Taking up the sweeps again they made it to shelter behind Popham Island. In the morning a passing fish packer obligingly gave them a tow in to Gibson's Landing, where they finally determined that in putting the engine back together at Pender they had forgotten to tighten up a set screw. All their cranking had been for naught. They got the engine going and made it into Vancouver's inner harbour with no more excitement. Dad said that through most of this

This photo, taken during the Griffins' time in Terrace, shows George at the upright Underwood, probably writing one of the little educational books that Dent published.

activity my brother slept under the bunk on an old blanket nestled among the tools and spare parts, utterly oblivious to the hubbub. This set the pace for his adult life, when he slept in his troller on the Big Banks, miles out of Ucluelet on the west coast of Vancouver Island.

In July 1929, when I was six weeks old, Dad undertook to find a car for Grandpa. He saw an ad for a Ford Touring Car and after some haggling, got it for ten dollars. The licence cost him a dollar and the freight to Cortez eleven dollars. We arrived at the Manson's Landing dock, where the car was unloaded to the entertainment of all assembled. Dad said the road was still pretty awful, with lumps and potholes along the way. The sandy hill just past the Bartholomew place was steep, with deep, cream-coloured sand as slippery as ice. He unloaded everyone at the top of the hill and got down to the bottom where the creek runs into Chris' Lagoon, but when he tried to make it up the next hill the engine overheated and the car would go no farther. My mother staggered off toward Grandma's carrying me and a small suitcase, while Grandpa, Georgie, and my dad lugged the rest of the duffel.

Dad had bought a tent from Ritchie outfitting in Vancouver, which he set up under an old yew tree for our summer home. Aunt Bettie had been married to Dad's brother for some time and was there with my cousin Rod, so my brother had a companion. Aunt Nora took me to the beach on hot days and Mother set to work helping Grandma.

The touring car finally made it to the house, much to the delight of Grandpa and the consternation of his neighbours as he commenced his habit of rattling along as fast as he could go. There was another car on the island belonging to Mike Manson, who saw no need for a licence. When the overworked game warden finally presented him with a summons, Manson paid the $25 fine and continued to drive the car as it was. And Grandpa's car continued to get stuck on the hills. He got a geared winch and hauled it up by that method.

There were no more trips for us in Grandpa's boat. He hardly needed it anymore because he could transport his fruit to the steamship at Manson's a lot faster than he could take it by boat down to Powell River in hopes of selling it. The aging craft was hauled up onto the beach in

Reverend Alan Greene of the Columbia poses with June, who is wearing the family christening robe. The font was a blue china bowl from the Prince of Wales' residence where Alfred Hayes worked with the flowers. He was given the bowl when the set was discarded.

Ashford Bay for the last time. I suppose, in retrospect, it had served its purpose, because the misadventures on Grandpa's boat helped to acquaint my dad with the possibilities of managing his own craft, although he never developed Grandpa's insouciance about coastal travel. Having our own boat made a lot of sense because we obviously were going to be voyaging to Cortez frequently. At any rate, by the time I was a year old we were retracing his steps up the coast in the *Loumar*, with our own adventures yet to come.

4 BLIND CREEK AND REFUGE COVE

My appearance heralded the beginning of the Depression, and there was no more work for Grandpa at Powell River townsite. The loss of this income had a disastrous effect on the family, though I was unaware of it at the time, and several of the Hayes' daughters moved to the city to find work.

It must have been around this time that the gas-driven clothes washer arrived at Grandma's, possibly just after Grandma had left home and gone to live with her working daughters in Vancouver. Life on the farm and income from the ample crop of fruit was so poor that the future must have looked bleak. All the children had left home, so she virtually ran away, but Grandpa refused to leave his beloved roses and orchards to follow her, nor could he afford to do so. This scandal was kept quiet as I only heard about it from my dad when he was in his eighties.

Yet life in the city with the girls struggling to hold jobs during the Depression must have held no security for Grandma because she returned home. I wonder if the washer was an attempt on Grandpa's part to reassure her that life wouldn't always be so awful. At any rate, the washing machine with its foot-pedal crank, thrashing agitator, power-driven wringer, and Briggs and Stratton engine sang out a brisk *put-put-put* to let the world know when it was wash day. There was a long pipe on the exhaust outlet that led the blue smoke away and fed it to the tall, dry, raw-sienna-coloured summer grasses.

I was oblivious to the drama taking place, however, and remember our summer days at Cortez as happy times. Both my parents would set to work at the Hayes place, and Georgie had his cousin Roddy as a playmate.

Since there was good shelter for the *Loumar* in Blind Creek, and a sort of wagon trail that led the mile to my grandparents' place from the Roarks' house, we would always anchor there. Elbert (Ed) Hansard

Bettie posed Georgie and her son, Roddy, holding a pole across their shoulders from which hangs a fish George caught. Bettie would have done well in the fledgling movie industry as she knew how to set up a photo.

Roark was apparently a watchmaker by trade. He had come to the area as a bachelor and worked as a cook in various logging camps before deciding that farming hours beat cookhouse hours. He moved to Blind Creek and started up a chicken ranch on land across from the Aldrich place. It boggles the mind that a watchmaker should move so far from the city and take up farming. But old-timers jokingly suggest that he broke more watches than he fixed, so maybe the move was one of survival. He met his future wife, Elizabeth Graham, when she came to Cortez to visit her sister, Jean Williamson, who taught at the Seaford school. (The Roarks are mentioned in Beth Hill's book *Upcoast Summers*.)

At first the Roarks lived in a shack near the beach, but later Ed built his wife a larger two-storey house. The shell of it stood until 1994 on private land behind the BC Hydro storage building near the Cortes Bay government dock, but the winter snow and winds of 1995 sent it drooping to one side. Like all pioneer houses it made much use of peeled cedar poles with handsplit cedar shakes on the roof and walls. The house, which could be seen from the bay at that time, was set back from the water but near the garden and orchard. Ed and subsequent owners cleared much of the land that is now thick with alders right up to Bartholomew Road. In those days pioneers made sure that the forest was well away from the buildings because firefighting as we know it

Fraser Gavin (left) and his brother were Blind Creek playmates.
Here they sit on the rock breakwater at Cortes Bay, with the home of
Ed and Lizzie Roark in the far background.(Fraser Gavin photo)

did not exist. Like my grandparents, Ed had expected to make something of a living on the island but ended up like everyone else, scratching by and only too glad when the old-age pension finally arrived.

Mrs. Roark was a tiny lady who had been deformed by a childhood accident that left her with a severely shortened torso, but she was a sweet, kindly person and a most accomplished musician. Before she came to Cortez she supported herself in Vancouver by giving violin concerts, which sometimes involved playing to entertain on the cruise ship SS *Oriana* when it was docked in Vancouver after a Pacific crossing from Australia. At her home in Burnaby she taught both violin and piano and was busy enough to be able to afford her own Model T Ford. Her brothers, Ray and Hector, used to laugh and say, "Here comes Lizzie in her tin Lizzie."

After Jean Williamson left her teaching job on Cortez Island, her children would come back up on the Union Steamship in the summer to visit the Roarks. Evelyn (Williamson) McIntosh remembers going out fishing with her aunt and uncle in Ed's long double-ended rowboat (which he called "the Titanic"), with Lizzie playing a ukulele and Ed singing a jolly song popular at the time: "The cat came back the very next day." One would think that Mrs. Roark would miss the income

Blind Creek and Refuge Cove

and honours she had received as a musician in the city, but Evelyn says she never looked back. Lizzie and Ed enjoyed their music, played cards, worked at mending watches together under gaslight, and shared the farm chores until her early death at 55. Ed went on to be 93. Both these pioneers lie together in the cemetery at the end of Bartholomew Road, along with my dear Great-Uncle Arthur Ashford.

We anchored the *Loumar* just down the bay from Roarks' house so we would be near the trail to my grandparents' house. But the first order of the day, before visiting and work, was a naked bath in the salt chuck for my parents while the coffee percolated on the stove. (By the time we got out of bed, the bay was virtually empty of the few fishing boats that anchored there.) Then my brother and I took our turns to climb down the rope ladder. Strangely enough, I don't remember the water being exceptionally cold. I suspect regular exposure made the body immune to the chill. Hot tub baths were something that waited until we returned to the city in the fall. The first saltwater soap we found to use on the boat was a grey, sandy product that lathered grudgingly. It was not available in the early years, so we took baths to rinse off the sweat and transfer the remaining dirt to towels that had to be handwashed.

Dad had found an excellent source of water to haul to the boat. The stream was beside the trail (Papp Road) that led up the hill to Harry Daniels' pasture. I can remember rowing ashore with him and manfully (womanfully?) grabbing the other side of the bucket handle in order to keep his leg from being banged. (He had awesome varicose veins left over from route marches in tight puttees when he was in army training at Edmonton in 1916. The damage was enough to earn him a medical discharge and send him into teacher training while his buddies went overseas to get gassed or killed in the long nasty land war in Europe.) Together we would struggle the pails into the rowboat and were lucky if we got most of the water onto the *Loumar* where the laundry waited.

Our clothing needs were necessarily simple and in dark colours. Mother and I lived in shorts and handmade halters, a sort of triangular gesture toward modesty. As my mother had a lovely figure, I'm sure my dad appreciated this attire. For us children, shoes waited until we went back to city streets, when we also had the fascinating experience of seeing the bottoms of our feet shed the hard-won calluses of a barefoot summer. The island roads were easy on the feet as they consisted of two dirt tracks with grass in the middle and trees meeting overhead. Since electricity and telephones had not come to the island, there was no

The Refuge Cove dock in 1924 with the fish-buying scow belonging to the Fishermen's Co-op. Beside it is the lean-to where freight offloaded from the steamships was stored. The USS Chelosin is just pulling in. This photo was taken by Sydney Taylor, Refuge Cove schoolteacher. (BCARS H-04043)

need for the wide setback of today's roads, where the summer sun bakes you as you trudge along. Barefoot walking on beaches was possible because today's sharp-edged oysters, which were imported from Japan and planted in Pendrell Sound, had not yet acclimatized and spread. The rare native oyster was a small, rock-clinging disc, so the worst things our feet had to deal with were broken clamshells and small barnacles upon which it was a matter of pride to walk without wincing. Also, beaches were not littered with broken bottles, and plastic had yet to be invented.

We considered the ocean our garbage disposal system, but all the trash was biodegradable so we seldom saw anything on the beaches that was not natural. Housewives reused jars for preserving food. Peanut butter and other condiments were available in bottles if you supplied the container; otherwise most things came in cans that were made of tin and quickly rusted away on the ocean bottom. With no refrigeration available we used up what we had while it was fresh.

All baked goods consumed by upcoast pioneers were made at home. In those days yeast had not yet been dehydrated, so it came in soft perishable cubes. Most pioneers bypassed this issue by keeping a jar of sourdough working, but Mother wanted the yeast cakes. When we were in the city we ate store-made bread from either the bakers or the Piggly-Wiggly grocers, so maybe she hadn't developed the habit of using the home-brewed variety. Or perhaps she just wanted to ensure

In 1932 George lugs groceries from Fishermen's Co-op Store at Refuge Cove, his chic celluloid sun visor slightly atilt. Georgie, Nerine, and June perch on the steps while Marjorie looks on.

a regular outing to Refuge Cove on West Redonda Island. As the years went by and cousins accumulated in Blind Creek, these shopping trips became social occasions, as there were always passengers to take along.

The first Refuge Cove that I knew consisted of a store on land, built of wood, with living quarters in the back room. There was fuel and water available there, a freight shed for the Union Steamships, and an ice-filled fish-buying barge tied up near the outer end of the single dock. These barges belonged to the fishing companies. At the end of the season they were usually towed to the city, where they were stored along the sides of the Fraser River for the winter. The earliest photo I have shows my dad on the steps of the store in about 1932.

Eddy Moyer and Fred Veander had owned the business for a time. They ran a good-sized fish packer called the *Resort*, which was built like an East Coast boat with the piloting cabin well aft. They would go out in this boat to pick up fish directly from the rowboat fishermen. The fish were brought back to the barge and packed in ice, where they awaited pickup by the large transport packer. During Moyer and Veander's ownership there were dances held in the large room at the back of the store. To get to the hall you walked along the covered veranda that ran the length of the building on the ocean side.

Nellie (Smith) Jeffery, who grew up in the tiny settlement of Seaford on Cortez across from Refuge Cove, said that as children she and her sisters rowed their salmon catch all the way across from Cortez to sell to the fish buyer at Refuge. She also remembers as a teenager having great fun at the dances. That was before Jack Tindall bought the business and converted the hall into commodious living quarters.

According to Bill Emery, an old-timer who grew up in Pendrell Sound on East Redonda Island, Mr. Tindall arrived at Refuge Cove from working in the store at Stuart Island. He'd heard that Moyer and Veander had gone bank-

Jack Tindall ran the Refuge Cove store for several years before going into business with Jim Spilsbury. (Maryann McCoy photo)

rupt and that the works had gone into receivership. Jack had a total of $25 in his pocket, but he had the drive to make a go of things and was unlikely to drink up all the profits. The receivers gave him six months to turn things around. With that encouragement Jack got to work. Besides being a hard worker, he was an astute businessman who was open to new ideas and was an all-around capable man, a spare, fine-looking gentleman who never seemed to get angry or flustered. For the first few years he ran the operation virtually single-handed.

Joe Christensen said that Jack would buy your fish, accept your produce for sale, fill your gas tank, and gather your grocery order, keeping all the facts in his head and totalling up the account back in the store. He always gave you full value if you brought in fruit or vegetables to be sold. Joe said that his parents grew strawberries at their homestead in the Salt Lagoon (Roscoe Bay) on West Redonda. The first boxes in the spring would go for 25 cents, and his dad always got that amount back in goods from the store.

Going to Tindall's was always a pleasure. Inside the store there was just about anything a pioneer could want. There were gumboots, clothing, fishing gear, general hardware, canned goods, local produce, perishable goods (if the steamer had arrived recently), and the precious yeast cakes. Occasionally these had been poorly handled at some point in their short life and were mouldy and unusable, but most of the time they lived up to Mother's expectations.

We never saw Mrs. Tindall behind the counter. She was not involved in running the store but remained detached, looking after her little girl and longing for life in the city. In time she became quite unwell, so Mr. Tindall hired Jack Parry to help with the work. It was a busy place with settlers, handloggers, and fishermen relying on the regular arrival of supplies. The Parrys, who had previously worked at Egmont, brought a house that was set up on the rocky bench just to seaward of the store. Now my mother could visit with Jack Parry's wife, Lillian, who was a Jeffery and had grown up next to the Hayes place on Cortez Island.

I can remember the day my dad stood in awe, looking at the various tubes and wires Mr. Tindall had set up at the rear of the shop. This was one of the earliest radiotelephones, which kept him in touch with the outside world. Coastal radio was still in its infancy, but Jack wisely took advantage of all the help it offered. It allowed him to place orders in Vancouver for supplies or call for the fish packer when the scow was filled to capacity, without having to wait on the steamship to carry messages. No doubt Jim Spilsbury from Savary Island introduced Jack to this marvel.

We children loved visiting Refuge because the perch fishing was great. Most snaps feature a row of little bottoms, while our noses are pressed down close to the water. Perch are shy fish and require absolute stillness on the part of the fisherman. To catch them we used crushed black mussels for bait, but we had to thread the dark heart carefully onto the hook because the rest of the meat tore too easily. If we were lucky, and very brave, we might find a long, segmented, pile worm among the mussels. The worm could be cut up for bait, but these grey, squirmy creatures had nasty pincers that came oozing out at the business end when we squeezed them, so we always felt we were in danger of being bitten. Years later, by the light of the moon shining into the water at Minstrel Island one night, I watched pile worms swimming frantically around, spreading a grey film of spawn, and all the while being gobbled up by shiners, so I guess the fish get their innings eventually.

Perch are one of the few fish that bear live infants. One year at Refuge Cove there was a pet baby black bear called Bingo who would come squealing down the dock to eat the embryonic perch that we

Bingo, the bear, gets a feed of baby perch from
Rod and Georgie at Refuge Cove, c. 1933.

obligingly squeezed out of the pregnant mother fish. Bingo ended up
at the Stanley Park Zoo when he grew large and began climbing onto
other people's boats looking for food, but his first love as a baby was our
little fish.

The best view of marine life under any dock was to be had between
your legs as you sat patiently on the seat of the privy that hung out over
the far end of most floats in those early days. Children seem to have a
fascination for trying out different toilets. So it was with me as we
wended our way upcoast to the various wharves. Early pictures of
Gibson's Landing feature the tall, narrow building—its use probably
unknown to the travelling photographer who creatively included it in
his scene.

Mother often bottled salmon while we remained tied up at Refuge
Cove. It may have been because water was readily available there or it
may have been the presence of cheap fish. If the large packer that picked
up fish was overdue and the ice was melting rapidly, I'm sure Mr.
Tindall was glad to get rid of the catch that had been held the longest.
While Dad or Georgie cut the fish into slices, Mother packed them
snugly into the bottles. The filled jars were set in water in a large copper
boiler that was balanced on top of the trusty old Coleman gas stove out
on the dock so that the boat was spared all the steam and heat generated
by three hours of boiling.

Georgie and Marjorie canning salmon on Refuge Cove float.

A round of canning was usually followed by a swim. We were often the only boat at Refuge because we were careful not to come on Sunday. Sundays were Boat Day, when the freight had just arrived on the steamship and every settler and handlogger for miles around was at the dock. With the wharf to ourselves and with a high tide coming up over the sun-baked granite shoreline, the water was warm and clean. We wore black or maybe black-and-white woollen bathing suits, as cotton was too baggy and fragile and other materials had not yet been invented. The boys had suits that came up over their shoulders like singlets but featured daring cutouts on the sides at the rib cage. These suits seemed to provide warmth even when wet and, except for the occasional moth-meal, remained intact to be handed down to the next wearer.

When suppertime neared we headed for home. We children sat on the top deck and watched for Plum Pudding Island to separate itself from the background. One wonderful day we gaped in awe as the first seaplane we had ever seen roared overhead. It was probably piloted by Jim Spilsbury, who went on to found the first coastal airline.

By 1945 Tindall had sold the business to the Hope brothers. With the money he got from the sale, Jack became partners with Mr. Spilsbury in the burgeoning radiotelephone industry, bringing to the company both his money and his organizational skills, while Mrs. Tindall got her wish to return to civilization.

FAMILY AND FRIENDS

The first of the relatives to join us in Blind Creek in the early days was my mother's oldest brother, Art. He and his wife Mary, with my cousin Nerine, came up from Vancouver and lived at the farm site where the Happy Ranch now sits.

This land was originally cleared by Jess and Sadie Aldrich. Jess had come to the Cortez area in the early 1900s with his parents and his brothers and sisters from Rochester, Minnesota. His mother, Mary, was a doctor's daughter and could handle almost any emergency. When she was growing up in Rochester, her father kept his patients in the lower floor of the family house because there was no hospital. His daughters became nurses and virtual interns because they were needed. Mary's older half-sister, Hattie, had gone to school with the Mayo brothers, Charlie and William, who found school a trifle boring but livened things up with their collection of small animal carcasses that they smuggled into their desks for dissection purposes. Hattie said that whenever the teacher smelled the end results, the boys had to turn out their desks and dump the contents into the wastebasket. These same boys went on to establish the Mayo Convalescent Home, where they employed Mary's sister, Ida, as their first matron. Hattie married a fellow by the name of Ed Wylie, who moved out in 1888 to settle at Burdwood Bay on Read Island where he built a store and hotel.

Meanwhile, Mary had married Herbert Aldrich and went on to have two girls and five boys. One awful winter in Bagley, Minnesota, the children went through a round of sickness that included whooping cough, chicken pox, measles, smallpox, and what was known as black diphtheria. With the knowledge gained from working with her father she nursed them all to health, but then her eldest child, a girl, caught pneumonia and died. After the winter in quarantine with all her family, she told Herb she'd had enough of civilization and they followed Hattie out west. When the school at Read Island closed, the

Aldrich family moved to Langley Prairie in the Fraser Valley before coming back upcoast to Cortez.

At Cortez Island during the awful flu epidemic just after World War I, Mary saved the lives of two-year-old Nellie Smith and her mother. Mrs. Smith had come home from the Powell River hospital with a new baby, but also with a virulent strain of the dread disease. Nellie says that Grandma Aldrich went out into the woods, found the natural product she needed, and brewed them a remedy that brought down the fever. She was in

Mary Aldrich, herbalist and healer, is seen here on a visit to Clarence and Etta Byers at Von Donop Creek. (Etta Byers photo)

steady demand from all quarters for her medical skills, but she also knew which cases needed surgical intervention. My friend Etta Byers regrets to this day that she did not ask questions and record the knowledge of this outstanding healer. We are now returning to the idea that the slow cures of herbal medicine are often more effective and less likely to compromise the total health of the body than many modern solutions.

Besides being a frontier nurse, Mary Aldrich also tanned her own deer hide to make moccasins for her children and sewed cotton flour sacks into underwear and shirts. Of the many women who came to the coast, she certainly ranked as the most likely to thrive. In later years, Mary and Herb moved to Centralia in Washington State where, no doubt, she went on saving lives.

When their son Jess headed out from Blind Creek for greener pastures in the early 1930s, my Uncle Jack bought his place. Since Jack was busy working in Vancouver, he offered the use of the farm to his older brother Art, who had been painting cars in Vancouver for a living. A combination of tough times in the Depression, migraines, and trouble with his breathing, the result of prolonged exposure to paint, drove him to leave the city. Art, Mary, and Nerine moved into the original shake-covered house that came with barn, well, and outhouse. They got the usual chickens and worked hard.

It was not long before Mary was expecting her second child. Because of a blood Rh problem, she went to Vancouver to have the baby at Vancouver General Hospital where the staff was better prepared to deal with the situation than those in the smaller coastal outstations. At that time most local women went (well ahead of time) to Pender Harbour or Rock Bay, both of which had Columbia Coast Mission hospitals. When Mary arrived home with the new baby boy, Frank, Great-Uncle Arthur decided to surprise the new mom with two young nanny goats. Goats were easier to care for and feed on the island than cows, and he kept a fine herd of them that provided the Hayes clan with milk, cheese, and meat. Frank tells me that his mother went into her bedroom one day and found the young goats happily curled up on her bed; Arthur got his gift back.

It was a great delight to me to have Art's family at Blind Creek because Neen, as we called her, was just nine days younger than I was. I'm not sure how much of a delight the Creek was to Mary. She was a city girl from North Vancouver. Life was hard on the island, but at least you got to eat—if the crops grew, the fish bit, and the deer were not too skittish. Mary used to tell the story of the day the game warden stopped by in time for dinner. After enjoying a meal of farm vegetables, meat, and rich gravy, he wiped his chin, pushed his chair back from the table, and said, "Mrs. Hayes, that was the best roast mutton I have ever tasted." Needless to say, it was venison. Nor was the warden all that dumb, for he knew what a plague the deer were in the gardens.

In the early years, pioneers were allowed to shoot one deer a month. One night my Uncle Art was nearing the house after dark, carrying a coal oil lantern, when he startled a large buck. Carefully putting down the lantern, he sneaked the remaining distance home for his rifle. When he came back there was no sign of the deer, and his lantern had been smashed to bits.

Richard Finnie had meanwhile bought land in the southwest corner of Blind Creek that is now used by the Seattle Yacht Club. This property had been occupied by Tom Haven, an old fisherman who erected a small log cabin part way up the hill on the west side of the

Dick Finnie's log cabin sat on the present Seattle Yacht Club site. A guest sits on the left while Mary holds Buttons with Bettie and Marjorie behind her.

flats. I don't know if he had formally registered the land to his ownership, but evidently he was happy to accept the money offered by Dick, who promptly named the property FirCroft. Dick Finnie was a hard-drinking, swashbuckling pilot from England. His father was the engineer who designed and supervised the construction of the Brazil railroad. Dick was born in Brazil but was sent away to school in England when he was six. He became head of the rowing club at Cambridge and often wore his old school tie. Dick had a small troller and fished around Cortez Island for a living. He also kept a little sailboat called the *Quicken* to remind himself of home.

Dick Finnie, seen here with June in his lap in 1932, became Roddy's stepdad when he married Bettie.

The Loumar *with her steadying sail sits next to Dick's* Euclatan *and a visting boat on the right at Finnie's dock, c. 1933.*

Dick married the third Hayes daughter, Bettie. She had obtained an annulment of her marriage to Joe Griffin when it turned out, much to everyone's surprise, that he already had a wife when he married her. Bettie raised her son Roddy at the Hayes homestead until she met Dick, who cheerfully took on the ready-made family.

Dick's family in England funded the labour and materials required to build a sweet cottage that still stands on the crest of the hill above the dock. You could see the strait stretching down toward Powell River from the dining room window. Bill Illman, the husband of Dorothy, one of the younger Hayes sisters, said he bought his horse Babe to haul the lumber up the steep rock slope that runs from the flat almost to the top of the hill. With a suitably long rope, Babe could be backed to the hill edge ready to pull the lumber up the skidway that the carpenters built. Bill said that four men working practically non-stop had the house framed and nearly finished in four days. The house was architect-designed, and all the lumber had been pre-cut in Vancouver.

Dick's family also provided money so he could order the fishboat of his dreams, the *Euclatan*. The boat was so heavily built, with decks planked in hardwood, that it nearly turned turtle when it was launched. All of his boats had classical names and they were all overbuilt and top-heavy.

*Roddy, with Buttons, paddles his
Native dugout at Blind Creek.*

Bettie and Dick set to work and built a winding set of stone steps that led all the way from the bottom to the top of the hill. Since the local stone was red granite, the gravel spread in between each step was a delicate pink colour. Flowers grew beside the path to create a ribbon of colour running through the salal. The constant presence of a dog and the pioneer need for meat must have kept the deer at bay, unlike nowadays when they actually come right up on your porch to eat the petunias in the planter. Dick soon had an expensive chain-link fence around the garden patch, which was located on the level land well back of the house. There was a lovely arbour entwined with fragrant roses at the gate. Like many Englishmen, Dick was an avid gardener.

Roddy's arrival certainly livened things up around the Creek. He was a totally fearless daredevil who soon found himself the proud owner of an authentic dugout canoe that his mother bought from the Native people at Squirrel Cove for a few dollars and some used clothing. In this sleek, ten-foot-long craft, Rod set to work methodically exploring the area. The caves on Red Granite Bluff yielded up a fine skull, which he promptly mounted on the gatepost where our flashlights at night would pick it out in all its eerie whiteness.

He got to know Walter Beasley, who lived in a beautiful little log cabin about a quarter of a mile up into the woods from Windy Bay and whose land stretched toward my grandpa's place next door. (When we spoke of Windy Bay in those days we did not mean Red Granite Bay but the next bay to the west.) Walter told Rod about an unusual skeleton in a cave on Cod Rocks. When Rod paddled out to the rock to check out this bit of information, he found bones that seemed to belong to a giant. The skull was all in pieces but the jaw and bottom teeth were intact, although twice normal size. Rod rowed a visiting doctor out to have a look. When he examined the arm and leg bones, he estimated the man must have been well over seven feet in height. Rod went back some time later to have another look but found that the remains of the skull and jaw had been removed. I wonder if the doctor told a dentist friend about it. In her book *Upcoast Summers*, which chronicles the travels of the Barrows in the 1930s, Beth Hill recounts how Francis Barrow grumbled about dentists removing skulls from Native grave sites.

Rod found another skeleton in a most unusual setting once when he was out attending to a trapline owned by Fraser Campbell. This particular line was between Blind Creek and Turn (Mary) Point. Rod had shot an otter, which ran up a rockslide. He followed it across the scree and below an almost inaccessible cliff where he came upon a huge rock with leg bones sticking out one side and a torso out the other. The skull was missing, but it might have rolled down the hill after the body completely deteriorated. Rod said there were three green copper bracelets hanging on the wrist, which he brought home with him.

Rod also got to know Mr. Roy, who lived at the head of Blind Creek on property originally pre-empted by Ed Livingston. When my cousin Frank was about three years old, his father found out that Mr. Roy wanted to sell his place. Uncle Art decided that it made sense to get his own farm, and Frank still remembers going with his dad and sister to talk to Mr. Roy, who was French-Canadian and liked children. He opened a wooden box, pulled out a brown block of maple sugar, and carved off pieces with his jackknife for both children. Frank said that candy was almost unknown to him and the sweet granular treat was a chunk of pure heaven.

Uncle Art decided he liked the farm, so the Hayes family was soon in possession of a small, two-room cottage with a lean-to for a bedroom. There was a fireplace that did a tremendous job of sucking all the warm air out of the living room. A window seat ran across one end of the room under outward swinging panes that hinged at the top. Before too long there was a radio run by dry-cell batteries that was always turned on for the afternoon broadcast of Stella Dallas and other perils. Since my family had no radio, on the theory that it would corrupt our reading habits, I sat on the grass outside and was totally mesmerized by these melodramas. I think, in retrospect, that I sat outside because I felt guilty about abandoning the family standards.

The kitchen had a wood-burning range, cupboards, and a sink into which a gravity-feed system piped cold water—which meant no more hauling buckets up from a well or drinking out of a communal dipper. The piped water came from a stream that ran practically under the house. It *did* run under after Uncle Art built an addition onto the side of the bedroom so that the children could have their own room.

There were clamshell middens beside all the streams running into Blind Creek. Native families came each fall, set up camp, ate clams, and waited for the dog salmon. These fish returned regularly to these small waterways in earlier times, before logging clogged the streams or exposed them to so much sun that water levels were too low at spawning season. Years later my mother wrote to tell me that these fish had returned to the stream beside her home in the bay. The fish milled around for days, waiting for rain to raise the level of the little stream. It never arrived.

The midden by the stream at the Art Hayes' farm was quite large, leading me to wonder if the early people also wintered there. When the slope to the northwest of the house was cultivated, it yielded a number of artifacts, not the least of which was a three-inch crystal. I know of two others that have been found at abandoned village sites around Cortez Island, and I learned from Joe Christensen, who grew up in the Salt Lagoon and went on to become a prospector, among other skills, that the mountains behind Atwood Bay in Homfray Channel were one source of quartz crystals that was known to the Native peoples. He got his information from old Joe Barnes of Toba Inlet, whose mother was a local Native woman and no doubt knew this sort of thing. Whatever their source, the sparklers I have seen that came from midden sites showed no sign of wear that would indicate their use as tools. The glints of fire from deep within their core conjure memories of longhouse winters. Who knows what miracles the shaman wrought with the radiant gleam from these beauties? To hold one in your hand is to feel the old power and heat stored within. For the busy settler, long removed from the magic circle, these stones became mantel decorations to be admired when company came and to gather dust in between times.

6 THE MAILMAN COMETH

L ife for settlers around Blind Creek was often a waiting game; if you weren't waiting for the cow to come home to be milked, you were waiting for the mail to arrive. Seaford, which was known as Smith's Landing at the time, was the nearest drop-off port for freight and mail. Before the 1920s the Union Steamship tooted as it neared the landing. Cap Smith, who was the first mailman and lived nearby, would notify the boat that a stop was needed by running a flag up the pole near his house. If it was after dark he hung up a lantern. When the ship had mail to be delivered to residents in that postal area, Cap would row out to accept the mail sack from the lower unloading door on the side of

Cap Smith loading City of Lund *at the Lund dock. (Nellie Jeffery photo)*

the ship. This must have been no easy task when westerly winds or winter gales were blowing out of Bute Inlet.

"Cap" Marion Smith was a particularly hardworking man who at one time ran a freight ship called the *City of Lund* for the Thulin brothers, who founded the village of Lund. Later, Cap Smith logged, fished, and maintained a small farm to feed his growing family. He was dependable and honest and is still remembered for his ability to cut down large trees with a falling saw all by himself. In order to support the other end of the long saw he rigged up an elastic harness that was suspended from his falling axe, which he anchored in the trunk above the cut. Most people needed someone hauling on the other end of the long blade to prevent it from drooping and binding in the cut, making it impossible to work alone unless you were both inventive and physically strong like Cap Smith. (You can see a medium-sized falling saw above the doorway to the powerhouse behind the Refuge Cove store.)

The job of postmaster would have been both a help and a hindrance to Cap Smith as it required his presence every mail day. No doubt by the time Mike Manson, the local member of Parliament, had renamed the landing Seaford because of the existence of another Smith's Landing, the postmaster was only too glad to relinquish the job. Either that or the new candidate had "pull," because in 1919 the duty and associated earnings were transferred to Harry Daniels, a World War I veteran. Harry had come to live in Blind Creek with his wife Margaret, who had been his nurse at the Scottish hospital where he was sent to recover from war wounds. It may have been that Harry voted for the current party in power, as that seemed to dictate who got these employment plums—the term "pork barrel" is hardly a current invention.

Because the hour of the steamship's arrival was indefinite, the Daniels built a small cabin on the shore at Seaford. It contained a wood-burning heater and a bed. By that time there was a small float with wharf shed, reached by a narrow walkway on logs that rested on the beach at low tide. All that remains to mark that era is a leaning piling to one side of Seaford Bay.

Harry Daniels was no stranger to the coast. As a young man he had worked on the seal-hunting boats out of Victoria. When the Boer War drew his beloved England into a conflict with the Dutch settlers in Africa, he promptly joined the mounted brigade. This service was followed up in World War I by a stint in the Fort Gary Cavalry, serving as a staff sergeant. Prior to coming to Cortez he had worked as a surveyor at Wells, B.C.

Marjorie at Seaford float where pioneers like Harry Daniels, George Griffin, and Grandpa Hayes worked on wharf maintenance. This was a job for the federal government that paid a bit of money.

Dad said there were rumours that Harry had a common-law Native wife when he lived on Cortez between the Boer War and World War I and had fathered several children by her. Remembering Mr. D. as a stiff-backed, remote, authoritative figure, I can't imagine him rousing enough passion to mount anything besides his horse. The Daniels never produced any children, but Harry might have taken a bullet in a strategic area during the war.

In the 1920s the Daniels built their first house down by the beach, about where the Papp house now sits near the big rock in the bay along the northern shore. One day while the Daniels were both away, the house caught fire and burned, along with all the trees and brush on the hillside. It was said that Ranson, the recluse who lived near Turn Point, was responsible as he had some sort of a grudge against Harry over a problem with the mail. Luckily the storage building was untouched, so the Daniels made it habitable. It was there that I first remember going to pick up the mail with my dad.

Mr. Daniels was officially the postmaster, but often as not it was his tiny wife who was seen striding along the trail, bent double under the mail sack. Margaret Daniels, RN, definitely wore the pants in the family—usually riding britches. Yet she fussed over Harry like a mother hen. I remember seeing her peeling the skins off his serving of broad beans because Har, as she called him, did not like them with the skin on. She kept a red setter and also a horse named Kisses that could do tricks on command. When Mrs. D. rode by on Kisses, everyone jumped to the side of the path; better yet, you climbed right into the bushes because horse and rider pounded by with Mrs. D. lying close over Kisses' neck to avoid being swept off by overhanging branches. You almost felt that a cry of "Tally-Ho!" was in order.

After the Daniels' second house, which they built at the top of the hill, near their orchard and garden, burned down when heat from the kitchen chimney set the wooden wall behind it on fire, they moved into the horse barn, painting it inside and fixing it up quite presentably. When we arrived at the former barn to get the mail, Kisses galloped across the field to meet us. We children were terrified of his huge feet so we dashed breathlessly into the house and pushed the lower half of the Dutch door shut. Kisses would push his head into the opening and whinny loudly, and Mrs. Daniels would chuckle and place a couple of sugar lumps on her palm. Once the horse got his treat he ambled happily away. Come to think of it, his wild charge upon our arrival was likely the result of his sweet tooth, not his interest in trampling us to death.

When the sack of feed grain for the horse and chickens arrived, Mr. Daniels would row his big clinker-built boat all the way around Turn Point and into Seaford to fetch it home. Upon his return to Blind Creek we could usually see him pulling the freight on a stoneboat up the hill, with the horse walking alongside. In later years he made the water trip in an open boat powered by a little gas engine, commonly called a kicker. Perhaps the horse needed a kicker, too.

Mr. Daniels became the lineman for the telephone system that gradually spread across Cortez Island, arriving in 1912 by way of an undersea connection from Sarah Point. At first there was only one outlet in the Manson's Landing area, run by the operator, Ethel Hurren. You could go there to call out, but mostly it was used to receive telegrams. When Mrs. Hurren moved away, Mrs. Petznick, a former schoolteacher, took the calls. In the early days there must have been youngsters running with messages hither and yon. Also, there were many occasions when falling timber took out whole sections of the line. I can remember seeing it loop from one tree to another alongside the primitive road.

By the mid-1920s a network of phones had arrived. The early sets each had a pair of dry-cell batteries for power. To place a call you picked up the receiver, put it to your ear to see if the line was free, then cranked a handle on the right-hand side of the varnished wooden box in order to produce the necessary series of rings. In time there were four "networks" on the island, roughly tied to the four steamship stops. Each subscriber in an area had a Morse code identity letter assigned to him or her. Privacy was an illusion because when the bell sounded, everyone on the circuit was alerted. Eavesdropping simply involved a sneaky lifting of the earpiece from its hook, although if too many people listened in, the message was almost too faint to be heard. If the weather was stormy you knew that the line would likely go down and Harry would have to walk the route to locate the problem.

Mrs. Daniels also had other talents. She was a typical frontier nurse, doing everything from setting simple broken bones to delivering babies. She was a no-nonsense caregiver but seemed to really like children. Each year when the wildflowers were at their best she organized a rowboat outing to Cod Rocks, just outside the bay. There she taught children the names of flowers, hunted with them to find the location of bird nests, and told them about the various species of birds. This was followed by a picnic lunch.

At Easter time she would climb the tall bluff behind her bay in the early morning and hide coloured eggs. The children and mothers all met at her house and went for a hike up the trail with her to hunt Easter eggs and eat them with bread, butter, cake, juice, and tea. The juice was saved from her home-canned cherries, and Mr. D. used to grumble during the weeks before Easter because he had to eat so many dry cherries. The promontory, the largest one to the north of Blind Creek, is still known as Easter Bluff.

Hiking into the heavens atop a stone- and moss-covered hill in the company of women seems, in retrospect, to have been almost a druidic rite. The absence of adult males on the excursion, the search for eggs (symbols of rebirth that predate the Christian era), the gentle, loving atmosphere, and the joy in the beauty of nature bore little resemblance to the homily-laden, sin-confessing themes of male-dominated organized religion. Perhaps that is why we children remembered it so fondly.

Although we lived in Vancouver, I did get to join in on one Easter Bluff climb. In 1938 my Aunt Mary had come to St. Paul's Hospital to give birth to a second son. The Rh problem really surfaced that time. The tiny infant, Robert, had to have a complete transfusion of blood and stay in hospital while Mary went home to her family. At Easter time my mother, the baby, and I boarded the Union Steamship, bound for Cortez. I had taken this mode of transportation as an infant myself before the advent of the *Loumar*, but I had not done so for years. And I did not travel this way again until 1947, when I went with three buddies on the *Cardena* to work the summer season at Goose Bay Cannery in Rivers Inlet. So far as I can remember, little change had taken place in the routines in the intervening years.

The lower coast ship paused at every port of call, taking a day and a half to make the trip to Cortez. At each dock there was a crowd of people waiting for freight or passengers. The boat had a large mast and boom with blocks, pulleys, and ropes that creaked and moaned as loads were hoisted from the forward hold in big cargo nets and swung out over the dock to waiting hands, then returned for more. After everything for that port was unloaded, the outgoing goods were taken on. Meanwhile, the local postman lugged off the bags of mail, which included shipments from the much-used mail-order companies such as Eaton's, Woodward's, and Spencer's in Vancouver, as well as specialty houses near and far. The waiting crowd trailed in the postmaster's wake. Some people helped with the sorting task, the sooner to get their mail and go home to do the chores.

For me, it was a totally fascinating experience; not so for my mother with a crying infant and not enough money to have a private stateroom. Fortunately it was not summertime, when excursion trips were sometimes so overloaded that there was standing room only until you were past Savary Island. The stewards that Easter couldn't have been kinder. They supplied us with pillows and blankets so we could attempt to sleep under dimmed lights on the upholstered settees in the main salon. They also stored Robert's bottles of formula in a big refrigerator, warming them and bringing them to us upon request. If we had been in a stateroom, with a sink in which to wash baby diapers, our assigned steward would have taken the diapers and hung them up to dry in the boiler room. Although my mother did not have this extra luxury, she managed to cope.

I remember the uniformed man who walked the halls and deck, playing a xylophone and singing out the calls to meals. There were always at least two sittings to each meal, which cost the grand sum of 75 cents. We went down a wide, hardwood staircase at the aft end of the boat, entering a wood-panelled dining room where we found our seats with no waiting in lineups as we do today to eat our plastic food. The waiter arrived at our table with a menu offering three choices in each course. He returned shortly thereafter with a white linen towel over his arm to inquire as to our pleasure. The food arrived on monogrammed china plates and was eaten with solid silver cutlery. The linen napkins and tablecloth and the separate oval vegetable dishes for each person helped maintain the distinctly posh atmosphere. It did not seem to matter if you were a pioneer or a well-dressed tourist; everyone was on best behaviour and was accorded the same level of service. (Actually, passenger categories listed Lady, Gentleman, or Logger. The latter were confined to separate quarters called the "glory hole," where they slept off the results of their town visit.)

It seemed like the voyage went on for days, but all too soon it was over. We arrived at Manson's Landing, where Grandpa Hayes waited with his infamous Model T Ford. People on the island still talk about Grandpa's driving habits. Apparently he drove at top speed all the time. Betty Jeffery remembers being instructed by her mother, "Now, dear, if you hear Mr. Hayes coming in his car, you pretend to be going the other way. Under no circumstances are you to ride with him." Mrs. Jeffery had accepted a ride to church one Sunday, only to land in the ditch at a particularly sharp corner in the road. If the seven inches of play in the steering linkage of the '32 Chev convertible I drove in 1949 is typical of cars of that era, I'm amazed he was able to dodge between the trees and over the exposed rock outcropping and arrive home at all intact.

I am also amazed that the car ever started. Grandpa would turn the crank that was at the bottom of the exposed radiator while Grandma handled the two little levers at the base of the steering wheel. With one lever she carefully retarded the spark so that the engine wouldn't backfire and snap off the cranker's wrist. Then, if she was lucky and everything worked, she adjusted the fuel flow with the other lever, all the while advancing the spark until she got things just right. At least she never had to worry about a flat battery—only a flat husband if the car lurched forward while he was bent down in front.

There was a hand lever that came up through the floor to the right of the driver. When this lever was pulled back as far as it would go, the clutch was in neutral and the rear brakes were on. There were three pedals on the floor, much where they are now, but the uses were different. When pressed to the floor, the clutch pedal engaged low gear. When it was half way forward it was in neutral, much like today, but with the hand lever thrown forward, the release of the clutch pedal engaged the high-speed clutch. To go into reverse you depressed the middle pedal. The right-hand pedal operated the transmission brake. It is no wonder that Grandpa drove like a maniac; his mind must have been overloaded with technicalities.

*"Dearie" Daniels, postmistress, nurse, and midwife
of Blind Creek, with her setter.*

That Easter we motored from Manson's to the homestead and
handed over the infant. My mother stayed at Grandma's and slept on
the daybed in the living room, while I went to visit Uncle Art's family
and got to sleep in the children's room over the springtime roar of the
stream that ran under the house and off to the sea. I couldn't believe the
racket as my previous visits had always been during the drier
summertime. We played with Neen's toys and I learned all the
wonderful things that children in a one-room school get to talk about.
She had a much broader education than I did, as the rural teacher felt
free to discuss any general topic that interested the children. It is also
possible that the radio gave Neen a far wider fund of knowledge than
I got in a newspaper-reading family, especially since I was too young to
read for myself and Mother's deafness precluded any dinnertime
discussions.

When Easter arrived we rode in Grandpa's car to the wooden church
that still stands by the Manson Community Hall. My mother sang
joyously, if not a little off key, beside her father. The service would have
been held on the date closest to Easter that the travelling Columbia
Coast Mission minister could make it to Cortez, provided he wasn't

called away at the last minute to run a medical emergency to the nearest mission hospital.

When all the formalities of the season were over, Mother and I joined the Blind Creek pilgrimage to Easter Bluff with Mrs. Daniels. Although she was popular with the children, the women found Mrs. D. to be a sharp-tongued person with no compunction about putting you in your place as she saw it to be. If she thought your dress was somewhat less than becoming, she minced no words. At a time when most clothing had to be ordered from a catalogue, one often found oneself stuck with a substitute that hardly fulfilled expectations. To be told so did nothing to ease the discomfort. Typical of the British horsey set, Mrs. D. dressed most of the time in shirts and sensible woollen jodhpurs that were sent out from the Old Country. Sometimes she wore knee socks and brogues; other times she wore her riding boots. As her one gesture to femininity she always had her curly hair tied back with a headband in the style of the 1920s.

In their later years, Harry and "Dearie," as she came to be nicknamed, retired to Saltspring Island where, no doubt, she made her presence known. Yet Cortez Island would not have been the same without her, as many a pioneer owes his limbs and life to the ministrations of this nurse/postmistress who bravely and vigorously forsook civilization to carve out a livable niche with her husband in Blind Creek. I don't know if she ever received payment for any of her work, but Harry's war pension and the job of postmaster helped pay their bills.

RELATIVELY SPEAKING

I n the family photo album there is a particularly festive picture of the *Loumar* at the Seaford dock, loaded down with happy relatives who have come to greet a honeymooning couple. Mother's older sister, Nerine, had married Ned Garvey, a World War I veteran she met while working in Vancouver. Ned had been unmanned by shrapnel and probably had a small pension, but the prospect of no children suited Nerine just fine. They spent a happy week with us on board the *Loumar*, camping onshore along with the mosquitoes every night.

The honeymooners on Loumar *in front of the Smith homestead at Seaford. June and Neen are on the foredeck, with Mary and baby Frank seated above. Marjorie, Art, and Mrs. Daniels are on top, and Georgie and Grandpa Hayes are perched beside Nerine and Ned.*

Our stopover at Melanie Cove was probably the worst. The honeymooner's tent was a mere rectangle of patched and waterproofed canvas, open at both ends, with no screen door or window that you find on tents today. Citronella, a moderately effective insect repellent, may have been available, but we had none. Even I, a seven-year-old at the time, can remember the laughter each morning and the scratching as the adults moaned about bites and the location thereof.

The honeymooner's tent.

Nerine, drawing water from a well when she worked at Keating, near Victoria.

We never saw another cruiser at any of our stopping places. To think of Melanie Cove with no other boats is beyond imagining today. Yet it was the usual thing at that time. There were handloggers and small homesteads in many places—in fact the coast was well populated in those days—but mostly local people used boats for hauling supplies, not as playthings. Native people paddled or putted by in their canoes, going about their business. Tugs worked up and down the coast, sometimes holing up in places like the passage behind the Ragged (Copeland) Islands while they waited for calm weather. Fish-buying scows anchored in nooks with their load of ice, waiting for small trollers and rowboat fishermen to arrive with their catch. Fish packers came and went. The Union Steamships threaded through

Summer anchorage in Melanie Cove. The orchard in the background is where "Mike" invited Muriel Wylie Blanchet's children to pick windfall apples when they visited some years earlier. Mike was Andrew Suttler, who became a book-sharing friend of Blanchet. He had been dead for several years by the time the Griffins visited in 1936. After he died, a squatter occupied his house for a while but went round the bend and ended up being carted away by the police.

seemingly impossible passes such as the gap at Shark Spit. One that never ceased to amaze me was their shortcut to avoid Surge Narrows, where instead of breasting the flood they calmly worked their way through the maze of rocks to the east of Goepel Island.

As we explored Desolation Sound with the honeymooners, we stopped in at the Salt Lagoon, also known as Marleybone Inlet but today called Roscoe Bay, on West Redonda Island. We found why it was called a lagoon when we stuck fast on the bar as we tried to leave. Charts of the time were definitely small

When the Loumar *grounded in Salt Lagoon, Marjorie must have done her usual small washing. You can see the rigging suitably decorated in this photo. Beyond the boat are the buildings of the Treadcroft brothers' camp. George is patiently waiting for high tide to arrive.*

scale and there were no echo sounders to tell you the depth of water, nor were there cruising guides for small pleasure craft. However, boats travelled at a sedate pace, and if you grounded, all you needed to do was wait for the next high tide.

There was a small camp just outside the narrows of the lagoon, a logical place to build if you wanted the privilege of mobility. The Treadcroft brothers from England occupied this camp. Four brothers came west looking for adventure. Three of them—Edward, Earnest, and Arthur—elected to stay. With financial aid from home they didn't have to work, but they joined in the rowboat fishing life anyway, selling their catch to Jack Tindall at Refuge Cove, as did "Shorty" Bruce, who built a shack near them. The Treadcroft brothers erected a shed (which can be seen in the photo) and set to work building a 34-foot boat with a straight-up bow and a sailboat stern. It was partially planked with one-and-a-quarter-inch planks when one of their fisherman friends, Shaw, died at Cape Mudge. He had placed his fishing shack just below the high bank and died in a mudslide during torrential rains that hit that year. This put a six-year halt to construction of the boat while they puttered around and mourned the death of their buddy.

Edward was an agronomist and made the area around their camp a veritable feast of flowers. He was also an accomplished painter. My friend Joe Christensen, who spent his early childhood in the lagoon, has a number of fine oil paintings done by Edward. Edward's brother

Arthur was a civil engineer and was the one who designed their boat.

When I talked to Joe about our pleasurable visits to the lagoon, he told me that settled summer weather would give me no idea of winters there. He said that with all the fresh water entering from the lake, the inner bay became inches deep with ice when northeast winds roared down Waddington Channel. The most miserable boat-swamping winds occurred as a southeast gale began to clock around to the west. Then the wind would boil down over the narrow hill, suck the cold northeast air in from the opposite side, and make the waters of the bay frothy and totally unsafe. Joe said that his dad kept a skiff up on the beach in the outer bay. They reached it after much scrambling over the waterfall bluff, but it meant they weren't totally isolated in the winter. There is a picture from Joe's collection that shows wrist-thick icicles hanging from the flume that his dad built to carry water to an electric generator. With that much ice, no doubt the coal oil lanterns were back in use until the thaw.

In *Upcoast Summers*, Beth Hill includes a photo of Joe (Karl) Kristiansen and his two children. When Francis Barrow took the picture, Joe was logging and fishing, but in earlier times he had worked for Kingsley Navigation. Joe Jr. said that his father's pre-emption, taken out in the mid-1920s, included the land on the north shore of the lake, the stream and all the land around its exit, plus the property that now gives such pleasure to those who like to explore old home sites. The Christensens planted the fruit trees, ivy, St. John's Wort, thyme, and the lovely Dorothy Perkins rose that has managed to survive generations of deer teeth.

Joe's mother had had rheumatic fever as a girl, suffered from arthritis, and found the isolation and loneliness of the place totally unbearable. In an attempt to regain her equilibrium, she left for civilization. Joe chuckled about that term. He said that one day a visitor asked his father how far it was to civilization. Joe Sr.'s reply had been that it depended on what you called civilization. Joe said this puzzled him for quite a while. Obviously their place didn't fit the definition, but the bright lights of Powell River certainly qualified. On his next trip to that town, Joe watched closely and decided that the Anderson house at Turner Bay was civilization because it was the first house en route that was painted.

After Joe's mother left, Phil Lavigne came over from Laura Cove to stay with Joe and his siblings while his dad found another place for them to live as it was impossible for him to maintain the homestead, look after the children, and earn a living logging. Like most settlers, Phil had a gas boat that he used to go fishing and as his means of transport, so it was no task for him to come to the lagoon. Joe said that Phil treasured the written word, even though he could neither read nor write. He regularly got letters from his people in Quebec and he just as regularly answered them with the help of the Christensens or other neighbours. Among the orchard trees at his home site, Phil had an English soft-shelled walnut that Joe remembers to this day. Phil was a good cook, kept a clean house, and made outstanding wine that he gladly shared with everyone. In short, he was the perfect bachelor.

Today, a walk on the beach on the righthand side just before you reach the narrows going into the bay reveals two boat skidways cleared among the rocks, as well as a goodly piece of flat land now covered with young trees. I did not find the water source but I did note that someone had carefully cleared a walkway among the boulders above the high-tide mark so that you could move easily from boat to house with an armload of supplies. Even though I could find no sign of Edward Treadcroft's garden, it made my heart sing to find the cleared path among the rocks. But who knows when the pathway and skidways were made? Joe says that the Native peoples used this area for knapping flints into arrowheads and scrapers. He found the ground littered with shards when he explored it as a child. The river into the lake would have been the ideal place to net salmon in spawning season, and toolmaking was a profitable way to spend time while waiting for the fish to cure on the smoking racks.

During our visit those many years ago, we walked over Christensen land up the old logging skidway under the enveloping arch of young alders to have a look at the lake. On the way back to the boat, as we stepped carefully around the swampy spots, my brother caught a huge bullfrog that he tucked up under his shirt so he could smuggle it back onto the boat as a pet. The frog promptly repaid George's love by peeing down his belly. The secret was out and so was the frog.

We continued on our way, paying a brief visit to Mink Island where there had been a thriving mink ranch. Nellie (Smith) Jeffery remembers visiting there about 1923 with her father Cap, who probably had a contract to supply fish for the animals. She said there was a small cabin surrounded by flowers planted by the rancher's wife. After a stop at the house they were taken on a tour of the operation and walked quietly past row after row of pens in which the mink were kept. Joe Christensen says that when he was there in the early 1930s it appeared the pens had

One of Edward Treadcroft's paintings. (Joe Christensen photo)

Rui Shearman's sailboat Free Lance *anchored at Mink Island among visiting boats. (Daryl Duke photo)*

been taken apart for salvage, but the galvanized wire that remained was still in great condition.

From the 1930s on to 1967, when it was sold to the Nordstrom family from Seattle, Mink Island was owned by Rui and Isabel Shearman, who had a fine large sailboat, the *Free Lance*, and came now and then to visit my parents at Blind Creek. Like my father, Rui was a vice-principal in the Vancouver school system, but unlike my dad, Rui had been astute enough to buy a sailboat that did not have to rely on gas for go-power. He bought Mink Island when it came up for tax sale during the Depression after the mink farm went bankrupt, so there was no need to spend hours working to improve a pre-emption. This allowed Rui to while away his summers doing what sailboats do best: gunkholing hither and yon as the wind blew.

His very able deck crew at the time was young Daryl Duke, who went on to become a well-respected Vancouver-area TV director and literary critic. Daryl spent all his summers cruising with his Uncle Rui, Aunt Isabel, Rui's sister Winnifred (Daryl's mother), and Grandma Bertha Shearman. During the war years, when gas rationing caused cruising boats so much grief, Daryl bought a one-dollar commercial fishing licence that allowed him coupons for gas, butter, sugar, and coffee. This enabled the *Free Lance* to carry on cruising in between Daryl's bouts of catching fish. The extra fuel allowed them to wander into every waterway they cared to explore and to battle the currents into Big Bay

John Barrymore (right) and Rui Shearman showing off the wingspread of a bald eagle shot by Barrymore long before extinction of the species was a rallying call against hunting. The pioneers looked upon eagles as predators, in the same category as wolves or cougars.
(Daryl Duke photo)

on Stuart Island, where people like John Barrymore joined Rui in hunting and fishing expeditions.

Daryl said that his great-uncle, R.S. Sherman, who chose to spell his name without the extra "a," had originally come west from Ontario in 1890 looking for a writing or teaching job. When no work materialized he found employment as a surveyor's helper in the preparatory work for the Powell River enterprise. During a lull in the project he travelled in his canoe to Savary Island, fell in love with it, and vowed that someday he would own a piece of this paradise. Years later, in 1908, he came again on the Union Steamship with his daughter Maud and her cousin Winnifred. This time he purchased a lot near Green's Point from Keefer and Associates, a group of canny entrepreneurs from

Typical pioneer first home. Wilf Manson used this one while logging at Chancellor Channel. (Dorothy MacDougal photo)

Vancouver who had early on spotted the financial rewards to be had from that charming scimitar of an island. R.S. Sherman, Maud, Daryl's grandparents, Rui, and Winnifred spent the first summers in tents, but Daryl's grandparents later built a house that now serves as Daryl's guest house.

Doris Hope of Refuge Cove remembers the Shearmans coming into the store on their boat for supplies. She says that once, in its wisdom, the government department in charge of place names changed "Mink" to "Repulse" on the new chart issued for the area. When Rui arrived, the storekeeper decided to have a little fun.

"Where are you going, Rui?" he asked.

"To my island, of course," was the reply.

"Oh. What island might that be?"

"Mink Island, you fool!"

"There's no island around here by that name."

At which point Rui rushed over to the crisp new chart and stabbed his finger at ... "REPULSE ISLAND," he roared. "We'll see about this!" The name reverted to its old form. Since Mink, along with Otter and Marten Islands, had been named by Captain George Vancouver, it seems a trifle cavalier of the government to have made the change.

*The handbuilt sawmill where Georgie, George, and Ned Garvey
cut lumber for the Griffin house.*

In *Upcoast Summers*, Francis Barrow grumbles about a man gra-
ciously welcoming him to the anchorage at Mink Island where he had
been dropping his hook over many years. You'd think the guy owned
the place, he mutters. The guy was probably Rui, who did own it.

During the early 1940s, Rui employed loggers Johnny Thompson
from Refuge Cove and Harold Hansen from Cortez Island to remove
some trees. The harbour was needed for booming logs, so both families
tied their floathouses in Melanie Cove on the mainland, about four
miles away. One day Dolly Hansen saw Katie Thompson searching
around on the bottom under the float with a long pikepole. When
Dolly asked if anything was lost, Katie's reply was, "No, I'm just fishing
up the diapers." Apparently the crabs made excellent laundresses for
soiled baby wear. And when Harold told the story he added, with a
devilish grin, "And the crabs were huge."

After the honeymoon trip in those long-ago days, the Garveys pre-
empted the property on the north side of the entrance to Blind Creek.
This land went all the way from well inside the creek to the second bay
outside the entrance. They set up housekeeping in a tent erected over a
wooden floor.

Ned went right to work and built a small sawmill in the first outer
bay. Logs were floated around in front, southeasters permitting, and

hauled up on a skidway to the mill site. Here he debarked them with axe and adze, then manhandled them with a peavey up onto rollers where he could guide them over a circular saw. Pictures of him at the time show powerful arms and pectoral muscles—no Nautilus equipment needed here.

As soon as he had earned a bit of money he set to work building their cottage, which looked out on the inner bay at the site of the current house. There was good shelter for a float that meandered out in front of the house, making it easier for people to stop in and place an order—the islands were still without adequate telephones. The Garveys fenced off a small garden spot in the hollow facing the sawmill site. Remnants of the original fruit trees are likely still there amid the salal, unless the deer have finished them off. They lived there until sometime in the 1940s, when Nerine's persistent asthma attacks drove them to live out their years nearer to medical help in Pender Harbour.

OUR OWN PLACE

B y the time Ned had the sawmill in good running order, my parents decided to file for land in the bay. About 1937 Dad had found out that the land between the Daniels' place and Ned's was available for pre-emption. It had been logged by what we called the "Jap" loggers at the turn of the century. They took only big, straight-grained trees, climbing up many feet to get past the knobby lower trunk and balancing on what were known as springboards that were rammed into small notches in the wood while they chopped or sawed through the tree. Even today you can find isolated old stumps with the telltale notches from springboards because ancient trees were close-grained and filled with natural oils that made them almost impervious to rot. The skid road that served the loggers and their oxen was still evident, running back through the valley in the direction of Seaford. In fact, this was the usual walking route to Seaford to get the mail.

Dad set to work with the help of Uncle Art and Ned to fall enough trees, handlogger style, near the water's edge to supply Ned's mill. Some of these trees were used for the lumber needed to build us a one-roomed shore base; Ned sold the rest. Over the next few summers, all hands pitched in for the house construction, just like the old-fashioned building bees. I'm sure the blueprints had been drawn up during the winters with a little help from the library, where Dad also found plans for making a stone fireplace. He built a wooden form for the shape of the opening and worked his cement and stones around it, with the fire clay going on first. We had none of the usual grey granite on our land, so used the red granite that surrounded part of the bay. As the red stone tended to crumble and turn to rubble, however, the work involved a lot of carrying, sorting, and rapping with hammers until enough solid material was found to do the job. It seemed to me as an eleven-year-old that the job would take forever, as most rocks I lugged up the bank to

Children prepare to dance around the Maypole during May Day celebrations at Seaford School. Dorothy was the May Queen.

the house were rejected. The only drawback to Dad's form of construction was the lack of a flue lining. As the years went by and the fire clay wore out, the chimney became more and more hazardous. The present owner has solved the problem by inserting a regular metal chimney up the stack, blocking off the big opening, and putting a cast-iron heater on an extended hearth. (When you get right down to comfort, you can't beat a Franklin Stove.)

When the house was finished, the one large room with pitched roof and dormer window gave us a place in which to spread out, as George was rapidly outgrowing his bunk on the *Loumar.*

Now our land explorations really began. We hiked the bluffs and followed the skid road wherever it led. My mother told a story of the path to Seaford that kept both of us on the alert. In the early 1920s the three youngest Hayes girls—Nora, Dorothy, and Alice—enrolled in the Seaford school, which was built about half way between Seaford and Blind Creek.

To get to the school the girls had to walk down to the Roark place, row across the bay to where the Daniels lived, and hike the old skid road trail through the woods. They were in the elementary grades at the time and were classmates of my friend Nellie Jeffery, who now lives at Smelt Bay. (Nellie was one of Cap Smith's daughters and had been started in grade one as a five year old, along with an equally young Clarence Byers, because there were not the necessary eleven children to justify opening a school. No doubt that was also one of the reasons my aunties were travelling their perilous route to school.)

One night on the way home the girls stopped to look at two big, tan, spotted kittens that were playing at the edge of a stream. They froze in their tracks when they realized that these sweet purring things were actually baby cougars. Any advice they had ever heard about dealing with cougars involved moving ever so slowly, much as one sees when a cat is stalking prey. Alice said they crept backwards inch by inch all the way past where Papp Road is now, then along the rough trail to the head of the bay because they had no rowboat that day. When they finally reached the part of the trail that skirts the beach where the launching ramp now sits, they could see that nothing was following so they ran for their lives. Alice says she can still feel the sensation of her long braids banging on her back as she puffed along. They were late home and the story became somewhat garbled, so my Dad's version in later years was that the girls had actually played with the oversized kittens, not realizing that they were cougars.

The schoolteacher at the time was Jean Williamson, sister to both Elizabeth Roark and Hector Graham, who later paid court to many young ladies of the island, including my Aunt Bettie. As times were hard, Mrs. Williamson had left her husband working in the Fraser Valley and brought her three young children north with her. They travelled on the *Chelosin* and arrived in the middle of the night at the Seaford dock. They were met by Cap Smith, who gathered them up and bundled them into his house for the rest of the night. (I stand in awe of a young teacher who had the courage to travel with three small children, the youngest just three months old, and take up a job in the bush.) With five-year-old Hazel, three-year-old Evelyn, and her infant son, Jean Williamson hiked up the hill to her schoolhouse and the two-room teacherage that stood in the dark forest. When Jean found out a few months later that Jim Smith had a pleasant larger house available nearby with a sunny view and a safe beach in front, they moved there and she walked the short distance to work. (You can see the shore where the Williamson children played if you motor out from Blind Creek—Cortes Bay—and watch for a wide curving bay that opens up on your left as you pass a little rocky island on your port side.) To help mind her youngsters, the teacher had a succession of sisters and cousins come to the island. All of them, including Lizzie (Graham) Roark, ended up marrying local men.

As for my family, having a land base in Blind Creek changed our summers. Now Dad waited until we arrived at Cortez Island before doing the copper-painting, and I'm sure the air was fresher than at Clay's wharf. First he would work at low tide to build a grid of cedar logs weighed down by big rocks at each end. Then he erected side supports that stood amid the pile of rocks and were well braced. Sometimes the grid survived winter storms and could be reused the next year with little repair needed.

To me, copper-painting was synonymous with clam feasts, followed next day by chowder. While my parents scraped and applied Barnacle Bill, the bottom paint then in use, my brother and I dug clams. The period of zero tides during the day meant we had enough time for both boat work and digging up our dinner. With all the homes in the bay using outhouses and with few boats ever present, the salt water was clean.

The site was beautiful beyond compare. Red granite formed both the steep bluff and the gently sloped shoreline that faced the warming sun. Just above the water's edge there were two huge old fir trees that fed on the spring water that trickled down the gully behind. These ancient giants were already dying back at the top, but their gnarled branches still held a vigorous bush of needles.

The other change that came with our new base was that my parents were so busy clearing our pre-emption and putting in a garden that we seldom went for boat trips. To this day I regret that we were unable to wander as Muriel Blanchet and Rui Shearman did. Maybe that's what drives me now to spend much of my time gunkholing upcoast.

9 WE HUNT FOR A LOGGER

In order to meet the requirements for a pre-emption, we needed to clear some land so that we could put in a garden. The swampy bottom land nestled in the back of our place held out good hopes for a small orchard and vegetable patch. However, it was in deep shade much of the day because it was surrounded by large, straight, evergreen trees that had not been big enough to satisfy the early loggers. Now we had to find someone to take away our forest. It was a sad decision because the trees were so beautiful, but they also represented cash for my parents. We took one last ramble through the woods and set off for Von Donop Creek where a local logging "show," as logging operations were called, was working and where Dad was sure he'd find someone to take on our rather small project.

The trip turned into a working holiday. After provisioning at Refuge Cove we motored on toward Lewis Channel, gliding past the bluff and the heavy growth of alders along the Redonda shore that marks all that is left of the homestead that flourished there in the early years. The settler, Mr. Thompson, originally came to work at Black's logging camp in the Refuge Lagoon and put in a home by the lake that now bears his name (on some charts the compass rose hides this pretty area). In time he quit his job and moved his wife and children to the mouth of the creek that drains the lake. They soon named the nearby steep hillside Poverty Bluff. The kids older than six hiked to the school established by Mrs. Black at the Lagoon, and everyone helped out with chores around the place.

One fateful day Jimmy Thompson went hunting for a deer with his seven-year-old brother Johnny tagging along to keep him company. To get a better look, Jim climbed up on a large rock. He slipped, and when he put the butt of his gun down to steady himself, he dislodged the trigger. His horrified little brother crashed home through the bushes to tell his mother that Jimmy was all covered in blood, but he was so distraught that he could not tell them just where the accident had happened. It wouldn't have helped Jimmy anyway, as he was long dead by the time a search party found him. They buried him on the shore of Thompson Lake where he'd spent many happy days as a youngster. From what I have heard, the grave site is still there.

When the new school opened at Refuge Cove, the family moved to farm on the northwest side of the bay, where they planted a small orchard and grew much of their food. In later years Johnny Thompson took over the farm with his wife Katie, who was one of the Smith girls from Seaford and had met him at a Refuge Cove dance. Johnny logged and also fished for cod, while Katie went on to raise six youngsters. One summer I took Katie and her sister Nellie for a cruise up past the area. When I asked her if she'd like a visit to Refuge Cove for old time's sake, she emphatically declined with the excuse that twenty winters there had been quite enough, thank you.

On our trip years ago on the *Loumar*, we bypassed Teakerne Arm because we had made a special visit a few years earlier when Uncle Art was working there as a boom man. He would put in a six-day week, then row over to Squirrel Cove, walk all the way home to Blind Creek, and, likely as not, spend several hours hunting for the cow before he had to turn around and go back to work. One day he told us about a giant spruce they had received in a load from the Queen Charlotte Islands. It was over ten feet thick at the butt, so they had sliced a piece off to send to the Pacific National Exhibition. We hurried over on the *Loumar* with Art's wife and children, but we were too late to see the biggest piece. The loggers had cut off another slice to save as a memento to show visitors. It was like a giant water-lily pad. The loggers tied it alongside a walkway so that you could step out onto the pad and pose to have your picture taken. When my turn came I sat with my shoulders hunched in anticipation of it flipping right over with us on it.

This camp was located in the bay to the east of the waterfall where cruising boats now anchor. In the 1930s Kelly Spruce ran this operation and had its Sitka spruce logs brought from the Charlottes, half a million board feet at a time, on board the *Malahat*. When the logs were offloaded at Teakerne, they were prepared for inspection to see if the grain was straight and fine enough for aircraft framing. It was Clarence Byers' job to stoke the fire on a huge, floating, steam-

Marjorie and Georgie on a Sitka slice with the old ship Malahat *on the far side of the boom. During Prohibition the* Malahat *carried booze from Nanaimo to Mexico, offloading to fast lighter boats while standing offshore. In later years the old girl was outfitted with two steam donkeys to handle the massive logs from the Charlottes: one to lift them up and into the hold and one to drag them into position down below. Gordon Gibson Sr., the "Bull of the Woods," was her skipper. The stormy waters off the B.C. coast were no real challenge to either the boat or her captain.*

driven engine that powered a fourteen-foot drag saw used to cut these logs in half lengthwise. He said they left the last bit at the end uncut so that the logs stayed as one until the inspector came to select the stock. Then the loggers forced the tip of a peavey into the log and pried it in two. The grain was so straight that the logs would pop right apart and bob around in the water while the choice was made. A few of the logs were so huge they had to be quartered for ease of handling. Some of the rejected halves were saved to make platforms for houses and for sidewalks around the floating camp. Uncle Art said that sometimes when the loggers piled boom chains on them prior to making up a float, the log would flip over, dumping the chains into the deep water of the booming grounds and leaving the men to jump to safety or get a dunking. Since most loggers

Loggers at Teakerne Arm moving split Sitka spruce. Note the boom chain waiting the chance to escape. Art Hayes is on the right.

couldn't swim, and none wore life jackets, their wooden pikepoles must have come in for a lot of non-standard use.

The logging show around Cassel Lake, above the waterfall, was a huge operation. There was an incline railway to transport logs from the upper lake down into the lower one. A steam donkey engine hauled flatcars to the top for loading and kept a tight hold on the mile-long cable that controlled them as they made the trip down to the dump at the bottom. (The early engines had less than one horsepower so were called "donkeys," and the name stuck.) Then the logs waited in the lake with the floodgates at the top of the waterfall closed to raise the level of the water. When sufficient logs were gathered for a boom, or when dry weather prevented more logging, these gates were opened. Men bounded from log to log on the lake, using pikepoles to guide them into the spillway where they tumbled over the falls into a pen below, ready to be sorted into booms that were towed to the mills around the Lower Mainland.

On our 1939 trip we continued on past Bullock Bluffs to the tip of Cortez Island. Katie Thompson told me that when she passed that area on a trip with Johnny, they saw a huge whale thrashing around in the water. They edged nearer to see what the fuss was about and discovered that a monster octopus had a firm grip over the whale's nose and breathing hole. Try as it might, the leviathan could not shake the devilfish loose. There was nothing they could do to help, so the Thompsons reluctantly motored away.

Nothing so thrilling awaited us as we rounded the point and headed for an anchorage near the rapids in Von Donop Creek to dig and bottle the big butter clams that thrive there beside the active water. Mother set up the Coleman stove on the back deck. None of the pioneers shucked the clams before cooking because much of the flavour in the broth comes from the shells. We would steam the clams open, then cool them down enough to handle them. Mother always packed the clams and their liquor in quart canning jars. During winters throughout the Depression we had clam chowder one night each week, served with lots of bread and butter. She had to put these large cooked clams through the mincer beforehand as they were decidedly chewy otherwise. We never bothered with the little neck clams for canning because their size meant they were a lot of work for little return. (The plague known as red tide, which scares people off butter clams these days, was uncommon back then.)

The flat area beneath the trees to the southeast of the rapids was not far removed from its days of use as an Indian encampment. There

June and Marjorie at Von Donop with butter clams to can for winter use.

Andy Byers and Herb Morrison stand while Ruth Byers and Wilena Smith perch on a stoneboat. These heavy wooden sleighs were dragged by horses and used for hauling rocks and heavy articles. It looks like Andy has some pebbles ready to give the horse a nudge so the ladies will go for a ride. (Nellie Jeffery photo)

was evidence of recent use in an old shack, dead campfires, and worn places on low tree branches. Dad assured me these were made by papoose carriers, which mothers tied to the branches so their babies could swing back and forth. This information I have learned to take with a few grains of salt, but at the time it all sounded logical. In *Three's a Crew*, Kathrene Pinkerton writes of helping an old Native woman at Beaver Harbour thread cooked butter clams onto pointed cedar sticks so she could smoke them over a fire and preserve them for winter use. Since we were there for an obviously bountiful harvest, it is likely that the early people visited for the same purpose, and the shore was white with shells.

Clarence Byers told me that he had lived near the lagoon in 1925 while his dad, Henry, logged the area. Henry had come to Canada from South Africa with his brother Andy in 1906. They stayed first near Winnipeg, where they found work on farms. When their younger brother Charlie joined them, they moved to Langley Prairie, where Henry met and married Ruth Aldrich, Mary Aldrich's daughter. Later, Henry ran a livery stable while Charlie went overseas with the Canadian army. By 1916 the Aldrich clan had encouraged Henry and Ruth to bring their children—Amy, Margaret, and Clarence—and come to live at Cortez Island, where Henry and Andy got into logging near Seaford. Etta Byers told me that the Seaford site was the first time that pneumatic-tired trucks were used for logging on Cortez Island.

At that time George McGee, a very old, small man from the Squirrel Cove Indian band, lived alone in a shack near the entrance to the lagoon. Henry made sure that George got food when there was extra to spare. One day George told him, "Pretty soon mucka muck lingcod him swim by um house." Sure enough, in a few days George came staggering up the path through the dirt to the house dragging a huge lingcod at the end of a rope. Apparently Native people had traditionally camped at the rapids every fall when the lingcod came in to fasten their spawn to the rocks near the running water. Each fish produced a mass of grey eggs, enough to cover a dinner plate.

When I asked Helen (Hanson) Anderson, who grew up at Galley Bay, about the cod spawn, she said that the male fish hung around the eggs until they hatched. This would certainly make the parent easy to catch. They were simply speared from the bank, cut up into strips, and dried for winter use. She did not know of anyone eating the cod roe. Helen said that if you put an oar down near the eggs, the fish would bite it. The protective male would drive away anything that came near the nest. Nellie Jeffery told me that she had speared ling as a girl when they lived near Turn Point, so these big fish spawned along the shore in many places, especially where the water was active. There are currently fishing restrictions on lingcod, so maybe we will see a return of these big baby-sitters to our shorelines.

In the early spring, Native women placed fir branches held down with rocks below the low-tide line near the rapids when the herring were due in for spawning. When the branches were loaded with spawn, they were hung on racks for the eggs to dry. It seems likely that an earlier band had also used this as their traditional food gathering area, because the people that are now at Squirrel Cove have not always lived there. Most of them came from Toba Inlet after the terrible plague of smallpox had literally emptied whole villages. In the early days you could still see evidence of cave burials toward the mouth of Von Donop on the east side of the passage. This usually indicates the presence of a permanent settlement nearby. There was certainly room for a number of longhouses back beneath the trees by the rapids. This spot also met the requirements of a good view to seaward in case of marauding raiders, and there was an escape route either down the inlet and along the trail to Squirrel Cove, or through the lagoon on canoes that could be stored there in the event of emergency.

A walk under the huge trees near where George McGee had his cabin is a walk back in time. Today there is a picnic table near the beach, just above the dark earth that is speckled white with clamshells of long-ago meals. If you examine the huge cedar tree you will see the hollow up one side of the trunk where Indians stripped the covering away to get the fibres needed to make cedar-bark capes to shed the eternal rains. When the bark is damaged, the tree develops a dimple up one side that ruins it for later harvesting. The loggers call these trees "cat-faces" and leave them standing. Lucky us. There is another huge evergreen that had been burned out at the base, possibly in an effort to fall it before axes or saws were plentiful.

To the north of the rapids there is now a roadway up into the heights where some developer's dream languishes. In the mid-1930s there was still the remains of a sturdy wooden chute that ran all the way from the top of the hill on down into the water. There wasn't room at the shore for a regular log dump, which would have consisted of a landing area and about a dozen logs cabled together side by side to form a sloping ramp into the chuck. Also, the hillside was too steep for a truck or horses to control the run of the logs, so they were rolled into the skidway at the top and glided right down to land with a mighty splash in the ocean within a pen of boom logs. Only the straightest and best trees were taken by this method, and they had to be carefully limbed to make them smooth enough to prevent hang-ups in the flume.

If you go there today you will see the remains of a gas-driven donkey engine off to the side of the road. There are two huge, geared, cable sheaves, a spring with one-inch coils, and a big four-cylinder engine block resting nearby. I could not find a name on the donkey frame so could not identify the make, but an old-time logger would be able to. Nellie Jeffery tells me it had belonged to her husband.

At the head of Von Donop Creek is a little island that is joined to the shore at low tide. This islet contains some very fertile land. At one time it was covered in grass, which usually means earlier settlement by Native people, and peeking out from under the bushes you can find shards of discarded clamshells embedded in black loam. This was obviously the site of an old kitchen midden. A man by the name of Jimmy Layton settled nearby and planted fruit trees and his garden on the grassy knoll. It would have been easier to keep deer off here than it was in most garden situations because at low tide the mud flats made poor launching pads for hurdling a fence.

Boats at Von Donop caught in snow-covered ice.
(Scotty MacKenzie photo)

I met Jimmy's nephew, Harrison, when he stopped in at Westview in his fine cruiser during the spring of 1996. He is a coastal pilot and was taking a busman's holiday with his wife. He said that Uncle Jimmy walked to Squirrel Cove every week, taking fruit and vegetables to trade for bread and eggs from the store. He also picked up the week's supply of newspapers, which he carefully saved to read by coal oil lamp during the long winter evenings. If you asked him a question the following summer he could quote you page, line, and verse from the paper. Jimmy would have made good use of a lending library if one had been available, for he was profoundly deaf and needed the printed word to keep reasonably current on world affairs. He was a frugal man who figured that his expenses were about $28 per month. This included coal oil, staples, and his precious newspapers.

Jimmy had been severely wounded in World War I and was decorated for bravery with the military cross. An early type of grenade had landed in the foxhole among a group of his companions, and he flung his body across it in his efforts to get rid of it. The explosion tore a hole in his side, but miraculously he survived, as did his buddies. Harrison said you could stick your fist in the hollow of the scar.

Jimmy came to the coast and got involved in logging. He found summer work during the Depression fighting fires in the woods and wrote to Harrison's dad, Harry, telling him to come to the coast. When Harry arrived, the work crew welcomed him to the tent camp and

Von Donop camp, with houses mounted on logs so they could be hauled onto floats and moved. (Scotty MacKenzie photo)

said they'd take him up to the fire area in the morning, where he could earn the princely sum of 35 cents a day. When they awoke there was no sign of Harry, but during breakfast he walked into camp, covered in soot, and smilingly told them they wouldn't have to go to work because he'd put out all the blazes.

"You didn't!" shouted Jimmy. "Now we'll have to go up and light them all again."

Jimmy had settled in Von Donop in the 1940s, living in a floathouse pulled up on the beach near his island. In his later years he learned that he might qualify for what was known as the "burned out pension," which provided a modest income to old veterans. A young policeman came over from Campbell River to interview Jimmy and help him fill out the application form. The tide was coming in as they sat at the kitchen table, but the old logs beneath the house were riddled with teredos and rot and were most reluctant to lift their load. When the officer came to the question about living accommodation, he asked Jimmy how he would describe his surroundings. Jimmy stated emphatically that he lived in paradise, what with the huge oysters at the front door and his plentiful garden near at hand. The officer watched in amazement as the ocean crept across the kitchen floor toward the table where they were sitting. He looked down at the form that gave him a range of descriptors—all the way from outstanding to poor—then crossed out poor and wrote in "deplorable," at which point the building shuddered and levelled out. The water flowed back out the door. Needless to say, Jimmy did get his small stipend.

Maud Emery, who lived in Pendrell Sound and earned a living with her pen, wrote a fine review of this man and his little paradise in a regional newspaper called *The Western Producer*. In the article she describes Jimmy's meeting with the descendants of Victor Edward John Brenton VonDonop, the white man who first "discovered" this charming waterway. Imagine fitting a name like that into a government form!

We called Von Donop a creek because as you travelled its length against a tide you finally came to a large stream, just around the second to the last corner on the right. The stream was so wide and vigorous that it required a bridge for crossing.

When we were there, a logging camp encircled the bay. There was a rough road out to Whaletown as well as a wide trail to Squirrel Cove, which branched off from the main road about a mile from Von Donop. We anchored in the little bight to our left as we came to the end of the inlet. Since it was a hot day, George climbed onto the *Loumar*'s cabin and did a beautiful dive, only to shoot back out of the water shrieking "Jellyfish!" He had gone right through a school of the slippery, stinging creatures. Any boater who anchors in the same place today can view the descendants of these watery tenants who go about their slow, stately meandering under their gauzy umbrellas, completely oblivious to thumps and splashes from above. With the decided plonk created in these confined waters by untanked boats today, it seems impossible that we would have taken a cooling swim. But the *Loumar* was the only cruiser around during that long-ago midsummer week.

Next day we rowed over to the booming grounds of the logging camp and made our precarious way to shore along the bare, caulk-pitted logs. These served as a pen to contain the floating timbers until there were enough to make up a boom, and they were also the only sidewalk to the beach. The homes in the camp were sturdily built and were firmly fastened onto logs that were cut away like sled runners on the ends. When the camp was moved, these homes were dragged onto large floats and towed to the next site. The houses were finished as nicely as any city home, with porches, chimneys, and all the usual things except an upstairs. When we visited, the tiny hamlet of five homes stretched along the shore above the waterline. The houses were mounted on blocks of wood or stones, and play areas for children, doghouses, chicken yards, vegetable and flower gardens, and clotheslines stretched out to fill the empty spaces between the trees, with the evergreen forest forming a feathery backdrop.

This was a happy camp with close family connections. Clarence Byers lived there with his wife Etta, his sister Amy and her husband Scotty MacKenzie, and his parents Ruth and Henry Byers. Etta's sister Hazel was also at the camp with her husband Ken Hansen, along with Etta and Hazel's parents Flo and Irv MacKay, who owned what is now Linnea Farm (a co-operative venture that supplies organic vegetables to much of Cortez Island today).

Because there were large tracts of forest on the land surrounding Von Donop, the camp existed for quite a long time after we were there, changing its population several times. Eventually there were enough children, when you added in nearby settlers' progeny, to warrant establishing a school. However, when we arrived in 1939 it was a relatively new operation.

Ken and Hazel Hansen were married just before the camp moved to the site. On the morning that all the houses, logging donkey, and trucks were loaded aboard rafts, ready for the tug *Cheerful* to haul them to Von Donop, the newlyweds were nowhere in sight. When the tug announced its arrival with a toot, the group decided to leave a powered skiff behind for the missing pair. With much snorting, the tug got the long tow moving out through the fog. When they were parallel with Refuge Cove, the heavily overloaded little boat emerged out of the mist. Apparently Ken knew that there was no usable road out from the new camp, so he had borrowed a truck and bought all the vegetables my Uncle Bill Illman could spare from his farm on Bartholomew Road as well as those from John Manson's farm. While the tug kept them moving, willing hands loaded sacks of spuds, onions, carrots, etc., onto the floats. It must have been some hefty tug, because Etta said that they were at the head of the creek by three o'clock that afternoon.

I'm sure there were times during the long winters when this camp had its share of minor squabbles. It may have helped that the houses were on land, where you could walk off your peevishness, and it seemed to me to be quite unlike some of the isolated northern camps where suicides were not unknown among the unhappy women. The fact that most of the wives had grown up on the coast probably eased the strain, and the eventual arrival of a truck road that allowed them out for shopping helped. Certainly some of the camps we passed were far more isolated and likely contained city girls who had married loggers who bubbled with enthusiasm about the man's world they inhabited and never mentioned the total isolation and long, rain-soaked winters.

No one at the camp anticipated being free to log our place, but the men did suggest that perhaps Fraser Campbell, Hazel and Etta's uncle, might be willing to take on the project. They also mused that maybe Uncle Art would be interested, as it would put an end to his awful commute to Teakerne Arm. It took a lot of money to start up a logging operation, and we didn't think Art had any to spare, but we tucked the suggestions away for future reference and motored on to Carrington Bay.

OUR TRIP ROUND CORTEZ

Since the weather was settled, Dad felt quite secure about tucking into a niche at the head of Carrington Bay. Settlers had their hands full keeping a boat in this area in the winter, as it was open and exposed to northwest storms as well as winter gales out of Bute Inlet. We rowed ashore to inspect the remains of a shingle mill that had been built around the time of the first war by Bill Barrett.

When we got ashore we stopped to admire the gorge, cut through solid rock, that drained the lagoon. You would think that a giant saw had been employed to carve out this waterway, the sides were so precise. In fact, members of a Swedish logging family, the Norman brothers, had enlarged this passageway when they were working on Peter Police's nearby claim. The Normans drilled and blasted out rock to make the shallow channel deeper so they could take water into the lagoon at lower tides and also sluice large logs out through the spillway. Hats off to the dynamite expert who did such a precise job.

It is hard to examine the project nowadays because so many drift logs have accumulated there, covering much of the outfall. Vern Borden, who grew up nearby, said that when he was a lad in the early 1920s there was a double gate. It consisted of a long log supported by gateposts. Wooden doors hung from the log and swung in with the tide, shutting when the water tried to leave. He said the loggers had drilled into the rock to anchor cable fastenings that kept the whole rig from being swept away. This gate also had the effect of keeping the lagoon at a steady depth so that they could float out the big logs that had grown nearby in the fertile soil. When they were ready to raft up the accumulated logs, they locked the gates open at a high tide. If you go there today you can still find the rust-filled sockets where the gates were anchored in the granite.

Bill Barrett built his steam-powered shingle mill on the south side of the channel, with a new house nearby for his family. It is said that he originally tried to install a waterwheel to power his machinery. He had mortgaged his handsome two-storey homestead that stood near Barrett (Blue Jay) Lake in order to build the mill. With its well-balanced proportions, proper cedar siding, and fine central staircase the lakeside house impressed the Borden children. It was truly an outstanding property that included outbuildings, a log barn,

Peter Police on the right with his modified truck, c. 1940. Henry Finnie is standing on the left with his daughter Elaine. His wife Pauline is seated in the truck, and daughter Ramona is standing. (Richens family photo)

and fine garden space, but in time the home became a combined bunkhouse and cookhouse for loggers from the Gulf Logging outfit, and the usual caulk-boot decorations dimpled and slivered the wood of the front steps. There was no way such a grand place could bring in enough rent from farmers, not when so many homesteads were going broke and not with such a poor route to markets for produce. I'm sure Mrs. Barrett shed tears when she left it. It had been a happy place in which to raise her seven children, with many a fine skate on the frozen lake in winter and hours of work put into beautifying their surroundings, which included the usual varied orchard.

At the mill, Barrett had a problem supplying his steam boiler with water. He finally resorted to laying a two-inch galvanized pipe up to the Borden place, about two miles distant. Then he had to build a long floating walkway out into the bay so his crew could wheel out bundles of shingles and load them onto a barge for shipping. He was only able to sell about four or five scowloads of shingles before the low price in the market left him with insufficient income to satisfy his creditors and meet his payroll. As with many ventures in the logging industry, this small outfit was killed off by competition from larger concerns, a phenomenon that has intensified today.

The place where the old mill stood is now well used by kayaking parties. It has become a tree-framed, sun-streaked, green meadow where you can sleep to the lullaby of the waterway. The end of the rusted-out steam engine has been overturned and serves as a huge fire pit. But when we were there in the 1930s, the site was a scene of desolation with a tangle of broken two-by-fours, collapsed roof sections covered in weathered shingles, and discarded chunks of machinery.

Carrington Bay had been fairly well populated during the first third of this century. At the inner end of the lagoon lived Peter Police, a World War I veteran from Italy who had both a leg injury and a metal plate in his head. From his ample grape harvest he produced not only a wine but also his own version of fire water, called grappa, which brought him a steady stream of visitors. Sober he was a nice chap, but he was occasionally a noisy drunk who could be heard by all the neighbours when he went on a toot. Apparently he was a fastidious housekeeper and a good cook, and Vern remembered that Peter would invite the whole Borden family over for an elaborate chicken dinner complete with dessert and bread, all made by himself.

The Borden farm, where Barrett got his water supply, had originally been developed by Vern Borden's maternal grandparents, the Simonds. Mr. Simonds actually had a cattle farm near Victoria and was a butcher, but the lure of free property drew him north to attempt farming amid the debris of stumps on some outstanding bottom land. Their son died of spinal meningitis and when their daughter married Borden, the parents wisely returned to Victoria and gave up their dream, leaving their daughter and her husband title to the land. Vern's mother travelled to Victoria to be with a relative who was a nurse for the births of each of her four children.

Vern said that the land had been logged using oxen. The stock barns and blacksmith's shop were left standing, and there were still miles of skid roads on which the children hiked and explored. I asked him why the loggers needed the buildings and he said that each ox had its own stall in the big log barn. Also, the oxen had to be shod with double shoes to compensate for their cloven hooves. My respect for the smith soared at that point. Imagine asking a great burly ox to stand still while you nailed shoes onto its feet! It turned out, however, that the ox was hoisted with a sling so all its feet were clear of the ground. This made the job easier and left the animal without leverage for goring the blacksmith.

The Borden farm, started in about 1913, required a lot of manual labour as there was no horse to pull stumps or till the land. The stumps that were in the way were hand drilled with a well-sharpened auger that had a four-inch metal bit on a long shaft that was topped with an eye through which you slipped a smooth wooden rod for a handle. First you drilled a hole parallel and close to the ground, then angled another hole down to meet it within the bole of the tree. Red-hot coals were shovelled into the bottom hole and the angled shaft acted as a chimney so you could burn out the stump from the inside. This sounds all very well on paper, but you have to remember that the butts of these huge old trees had been left standing because the original fallers found them too tough and gnarled to cut. It is little wonder that most were left in the fields, thus engendering the title that identified these early farms: "stump ranch."

The whole family worked hard to produce food. Mr. Borden cured bacon and hams in the smokehouse; Mrs. Borden filled numerous jars with canned vegetables, fruit, salmon, and meat; and the kids regularly fished or hunted. Extra eggs from the chickens were preserved in waterglass for the season when the hens went broody and refused to lay. The huge log root house for storing food was built partly below ground to keep out the winter frosts and to maintain low temperatures during sunny weather. This structure lasted for many years after the farm was no more.

As the garden needed to be hand dug, and as row upon row of vegetables to feed not only the family but also the stock needed to be tended, there was plenty of work for everyone. Yet Vern remembers it as a happy childhood. They played hide and seek, kick the can, and many other games that are completely unknown to over-entertained youngsters today.

Household supplies arrived twice a year on the Union Steamship and were hauled to the farm by Bert Middleton, who lived in Whaletown and ran a small freight business with his horse and wagon. When the load of staples was unpacked you were lucky if a pair of shoes was included for you; otherwise you went barefoot or wore the ubiquitous gumboots in wintertime. Candy and toys were not part of the order either.

One year the neighbour on the land to the east of them, Mr.

Stoney, hired Borden to clear the last piece of land needed to meet his pre-emption requirements. Stoney had no money but gave them a Fraser River gillnet boat with a one-cylinder Palmer engine to pay his debt. The Bordens kept the boat anchored in Coulter Bay and had great fun going to social events at places like Manson's Landing that were not connected to the north of the island by roads. No doubt the kids had worked as hard as their dad on the clearing job so enjoyed the boat even more as the tangible fruit of their labour.

When Vern and his sister needed to go to high school, Charlie Allen of Gorge Harbour ferried them to Powell River and brought them home for holidays. After one year of this, with two more children to educate and with their useful hands away all week, Mr. Borden sadly but wisely gave up his ongoing battle with the land and followed his kids to Powell River, where he found work in the booming grounds. Cortez' loss was Powell River's gain as Vern went on to become head millwright for the paper plant, supervising the repair of all the machinery. It is likely that the creative play of childhood and the work ethic developed on the stump ranch contributed to this quiet man's genius with equipment. It seems fitting to me that Cortez became his retirement home and my mother's garden his pleasure. But unlike his own father, and my parents, Vern has adequate heavy machinery to turn the land into a well-kept park. Viewed from her vantage point on high, I'm sure my mother approves.

While the old Borden homestead on the north end of Cortez had no waterfront, it was near enough to the sea, with Carrington Bay just a short walk away. There were a number of other settlers struggling to make a living along the shores of the bay. One of them, Captain Sparrow, had built a home on the northern side of the lagoon outfall, opposite the shingle mill site. This is a place of rare beauty, with the lagoon inland and a superb view to seaward of Read Island and the Coast Range beyond. Captain Sparrow kept both a large boat that helped him earn a few dollars freighting and a smaller fishing boat. According to Frank Tooker, Mrs. Sparrow was quite an outdoor girl who worked their small farm, where they raised goats, and also enjoyed running the small boat herself in nearby waters, where she was able to catch a respectable number of fish.

In time the Sparrows had two children, Anna and John, who attended the school at Whaletown. Their mother rowed them across the lagoon in an old tin lifeboat kept for the purpose. One winter,

Captain Sparrow had to run his son down to Powell River to see the dentist. In order to make the trip a paying proposition he took along some goats that were ready for market. From what I have been able to learn, it appears the captain stopped the boat in the shelter of Harwood Island while he fired up the stove to heat some food. Afterwards the boy fell asleep in the forepeak. When it was time to move on to Powell River, the father shot a squirt of gasoline into the priming cup to fill the carburetor to start up the engine. This was the standard procedure to start a Palmer, but this time either the escaping fumes exploded or there was a backfire of the engine because the cabin interior was rapidly filled with flames. Captain Sparrow was blown right out of the cabin. He grabbed the fire axe and tried to cut through the forward hatch to save his son but was unable to get to him on time. The boat was rapidly being engulfed by the holocaust. When it became apparent that all was lost, the father threw the goats over the side. They swam to the beach on Harwood while he scrambled into the skiff and rowed to Powell River.

Someone from the Nunn and Hicks logging camp in the area of Carrington Bay brought Mrs. Sparrow to Powell River. People who knew her well said that she never recovered from the shock. The father's remorse doesn't bear thinking about.

The early Easthope and Palmer engines used gravity feed for the fuel supply. When you stopped the engine you turned off the petcock in the copper pipe that carried fuel down to the engine. In order to start it, you first opened this valve to fill the line. Then you shut the petcock again while you primed the little cup by each cylinder. Usually a one-cylinder could be rolled over by hand, but if your engine had two cylinders you put an iron bar in the top of the flywheel after you had rolled it to get the pistons in the required position. The spark had to be retarded so that the engine wouldn't fire too soon. If this happened when you had the iron bar in the big flywheel, the engine would fire backwards and you would not be able to remove the bar before it crashed through the floorboards. When all was in readiness you heaved on the bar and snatched it out as it swung over toward you. Then you reached for the spark advance and opened the fuel petcock to ensure a steady flow of gasoline. Backfires were a common occurrence.

The presence of raw gas fumes torched many a boat, especially when so many folk habitually had a hand-rolled cigarette dangling from their lower lip. In time the makers of these early engines

The Tookers, like other coast families, have many of their fondest memories tied to their boats. Frank Tooker's first boat (middle left), seen here on the tidal grid at Coulter Bay, later gave way to the Maudie *(top left). Ed's boat was the* Nelwin *(top right). Fish were often a part of the good times too. In the lower right photo, Bill and Pat Black of the Black Logging Co. (near the head of Toba Inlet) display their catch while Ed Tooker and Thelma Boyd stand on the boat's cabin.*
(Ed Tooker photos)

*Eliza and Frank Tooker in front of their original log house at
Coulter Bay, with eldest son Frank, daughter Bertha, and a
neighbour lad in the early 1920s. (Fred Reedel photo)*

produced fuel pumps that could carry a steady flow of gas directly
into the carburetor, but with money so scarce in the Depression, many
boaters still used the old method. It is quite obvious that use of a coal
or wood-burning stove coupled with this kind of engine was a real
challenge to survival. The Sparrow family, which paid the ultimate
price for having this kind of fuel system, no longer lived in the area
the summer we came to explore.

We bypassed Coulter Bay where the Tooker family had a
homestead. Ed Tooker, Frank's brother, told me about finding a
skeleton in a rock formation in the bay. The upper and lower incisors
had the appearance of being double. I asked him if he thought that
was the result of the person eating a lot of sand with the clams and
wearing the teeth down. He said he had asked the curators of the
Cape Mudge Museum about it, and they said that some local Natives
had what are called double teeth. Ed's sister Bertha was studying
high school by correspondence at the time, and she gathered up the
skeleton to use in a science project. I suspect Mama Tooker quietly
disposed of it after the interest waned, because Ed never saw it again.
Mr. Tooker was away following painting jobs much of the time, so
Mrs. Tooker got busy organizing a library for Whaletown. The
building that houses the library is dedicated to her memory, and she,
her husband, and daughter are all tucked away in the graveyard near
Sawmill Road, just off Ferry Road.

Dad told us about the next cove that we passed after Coulter Bay. It was named after Charlie Strange, the Englishman who built a sawmill there. He had installed a steam engine, which was a considerable expense. He also needed to have a house built to accommodate himself and his two sisters. This used up all his inheritance, so he was left with no reserve of cash. The Strange Bay mill operated for about ten years but was never very successful because, being short of funds, Charlie often did not have a ready supply of logs to fill a lumber order.

His sisters helped out. Alice kept house. Old-timers still rave about the wonderful Christmas pudding that she brought each year to the party held at Whaletown. The other sister, Paddy, fired the boiler in the mill. Had she remained in England, Paddy would have been an obvious misfit, but she found her place toiling away at the mill.

Charlie lived until he was about 60 years of age. One fall he rowed across to Read Island to hunt deer. When he didn't return, Alice enlisted help from the neighbours, but a search party found only his rowboat.

His two spinster sisters had no choice but to stay on after he died. They made some money by selling the mill equipment to a man from Powell River, but with no dependable income, life was not easy for them, especially since the house was in total shade all winter and the northeast winds howled right through it. In time, the back of the house literally rotted away from the constant moisture seeping down the bluff at the back. Frank Tooker remembers falling a big fir tree on the property for them. He and Jack Munro dropped the tree and bucked it up with a Wee MacGregor saw like my grandpa's, all for two dollars each. That was fairly good money for a teenager in those days, but the brutally heavy saw must have been a chore to carry.

The Reverend Alan Greene was a regular visitor, providing at-your-door church services and occasionally doing shopping for them. He said they always welcomed him warmly and provided tea after the service. He lugged his folding pump organ, Little Jimmy, off the mission boat, rowed it ashore, and played it by ear, singing mightily to make up for the frailty of the other singers. I'm sure these two women looked forward to his visits.

Years later Reverend Greene told my father a story about the Strange sisters. I have seen it somewhere in print, but I clearly remember hearing it from my father when I was about twelve years old. On one visit, one sister drew the minister aside. In an embarrassed, halting manner she asked if he would be so good as to stop at Spencer's store when next he was in Vancouver and order some long woollen underwear in the ladies department. (In those days you could still get the most gossamer British woollen underthings for women, no doubt a necessity in the usual underheated British household.) It was to be a surprise gift for her sister, so she couldn't write out the order herself.

In due time Greene placed the order in the busy lingerie department at Spencer's and thought no more of it. When next he called on the household, however, no one answered his knock. He thought this odd, as they were never away. He thumped again only to be told rather frostily through the closed door, "We are not at home." He persisted because by now he was really worried about their well-being. Finally he was admitted to the living room where they stood with pursed lips and downcast eyes. After much pleading on his part he was shown a parcel: the package from Spencer's. The box was not unpacked, so he hesitantly opened the tissue…to be confronted with what was obviously a bride's undergarments for an elaborate trousseau! Greene was suitably shocked and hastened to assure them that being a masher was the farthest thing from his mind. Eventually he conducted the service and tea was served. It was not until he was rowing out to his boat that an awful thought struck him. What about the poor upcoast bride going on her honeymoon in her prim British woollens?

After passing Strange Bay we made a lunch stop at what we called the Camp Islands, now known as the Subtle Islands. At one time there was a hotel here owned by Mose Ireland, who was well known for his phenomenal ability to cruise a logging claim. He could go ashore, do a brief walkabout, and tell you with great accuracy how many board feet of logs you could reasonably expect to harvest. Mose built his hotel when he saw the need for temporary accommodation for the huge crews of loggers that came north on the old steamer *Comox*. The men were offloaded at his place and at hotels in places like Evans Bay. There they waited for the camp tenders to come and pick them up.

The hotel at Camp Island was not licensed to sell booze, which may explain why Mose Ireland did not make a fortune. Loggers seemed to have an unquenchable thirst, but in the early days even the steamships, though they had onboard bars, could not serve any liquor while in a port. To get around this regulation the loggers waited at a disused float on one side of Evans Bay. On any Sunday about 50 of them would dutifully board the steamer, pay a fare, and head for the bar while the skipper dawdled along, taking an hour to cross to the opposite side of the bay where there would be a staggering offload of inebriated passengers.

Loggers on their way back up to camp usually had spent all their money at Vancouver's watering holes. The camp paymaster would give them their money just before they left for town after snows had shut down the camps. The loggers would often arrive at the bright lights only to be set up by a woman so that her partner could steal the fat roll of bills. The saddened logger would wake up in some skid-road hotel with a hangover, the rent to pay, and nothing to live on until the next boat left for camp. In retrospect, handing out the salary in a lump sum was one way to guarantee that the workers went through it quickly and headed back to the exhausting, sweaty work and the months of isolation needed before they were bankrolled to do it all over again.

Speaking of booze, one Read Island hotelier, who shall go unnamed, had a lucrative sideline. He hired Wally Aldrich to boat up Toba Inlet and sell boxes of apples, priced at either two or ten dollars a box. It was not until years later that Wally found out why the Native buyers much preferred the ten-dollar boxes. Under all the fruit, bottles of bootlegged booze were neatly snuggled, awaiting the wise purchaser. Since it was illegal to sell liquor to Natives, it was cunning of the hotel owner to send a twelve-year-old out peddling his wares. Not only would the boy be an unlikely suspect, but he would also be too young to face the severe penalty that an adult would receive. I was amazed to learn that this lad was actually operating a steam-powered launch as he wound his way up Toba Inlet, stopping and starting at many little settlements and eventually wending his way back to Read Island.

The old hotel on Camp Island had burned some years before our visit, but twisted pots, kettles, and bits of china along with the chimney were still in evidence. The view must have been gorgeous, as the hotel sat on the north side of the tumbolo of gravel that stretched between the two islands.

Mose is buried at a lovely old homestead at Bold Point on Quadra Island, where he farmed and lived out his last years. Doris Anderson, in her fine book *Evergreen Islands*, devotes several pages to Mose Ireland. She reports that his death in 1913 was actually an unsolved murder.

After Mose was gone, his farm was operated by the Bell family, which shipped meat and produce out each week to Elk Bay Logging on Vancouver Island. The current owner, who cares for the fine old fruit trees with loving kindness, is none other than Joe Christensen, who spent his childhood nurturing the trees at the Salt Lagoon.

The second Camp Island became the site of a summer residence for Mr. R. Kerr Houlgate during the period between World War I and the Depression. According to Rushton in *Whistle up the Inlet*, Houlgate was a real estate executive and had been the manager of Yorkshire and Canada Trust before becoming a director, and later the chairman, of Union Steamships. Until recently there was evidence of a clearing with overgrown fruit trees where he lived. There is a report in a pioneer diary that Houlgate had a pig for sale, so he must have had a full-time farm worker on the place. With the steamship making regular calls several times a week, he'd have no trouble commuting to keep an eye on things. I learned from Frank Tooker that Mrs. Houlgate eventually became emotionally unwell, so she lived permanently on the island with a Mrs. Fraser as her nurse. Frank also said that the north island was where they kept stock and chickens, and there were small barns and pens there.

Around 1930, after Mrs. Houlgate left the house, fifteen-year-old Frank got a job through Mary Thompson of the Whaletown store to go and live one winter in the house as a caretaker. He said the well water tasted fine when you first drew it up, but after about an hour you'd have thought it came out of a cesspool. He and his brother Ed bailed the well empty. Then

Mrs. Fraser, the nurse, in front of Houlgate house on Camp Island. (Richens family photo)

Mary Thompson with Mrs Houlgate and her dogs on Camp Island.
(Richens family photo)

they tied two ladders together and Frank went down inside to scrape the well clean, right to the blue clay at the bottom. After all that effort the water tasted just as foul after it had sat awhile. He said the house was a pretty cottage, one storey with a white-railed front porch, a stone fireplace, good furniture, carpets, and a fine piano. Had he been an avid reader he'd have been content because the place also had a good library. Frank said he only managed to stay on about three months before loneliness drove him away.

It was not long before the deserted house attracted scavengers who carried away materials, including the hardwood that sheathed the floors, to build their own houses. Elaine (Finnie) Richens, who lived in nearby Whaletown during the 1930s, said that fishermen even removed the piano wire to incorporate it in their gear.

Nowadays an American owns both islands and has had comfortable homes built for his family and the resident caretaker. He has gone to considerable expense to bring electric power onto the island and has brought in the local water witcher, Duane Campbell, to determine if there is enough water to supply two households as well as the family riding horses. I can't help but wonder how the water smells.

Bert Middleton and Len Richens pose atop their mountain at the Whaletown dock. (Fred Reedel photo)

The old dock that served the Houlgate place was made with sturdy gumwood pilings and was located where the new wharf has been built. Blue gum, as it was also known, came back from places like Australia as ballast in empty freight boats, and the steamship company made good use of it. For years after the float went out, the local people dredged up the old pilings and ripsawed them into thin planks to use as sheathing on their boat hulls. Since gumwood was impervious to teredo worms and rot, the rescued pilings were as good as new when you cleaned away the outer muck. Although I am quite certain that the replacement pilings will not be as durable, I hope the new float will resist the winter storms and last longer than most have done on that exposed pair of little islands.

BACK HOME AGAIN

On our trip around Cortez in the summer of 1939 we stopped briefly at Whaletown, which had a dock where freight could be offloaded from the Union Steamships. When we visited there was a store at the dock, but in earlier days there was just a little shop in the Thompson house up the road. You could buy tobacco and small stuff there. Later, Mr. Thompson and his wife Mary built the store where it is today. They continued to maintain an active farm that extended from the head of the lagoon all the way past where the road to the ferry now runs.

Whaletown wharf and surroundings in 1909. Now this vista is filled with handsome trees and houses. In the 1890s there was a wharf built farther into the bay, with a rough-and-ready trading post and salon on shore. There appears to be no pictorial record of this first incarnation.
(Margaret Schindler photo)

Bill Robinson regularly took out hunting and fishing parties that set up camp right in the Thompsons' orchard. (Richens family photo)

The Thompsons were childless, and their only helper was Bill Robinson, so they travelled to New Westminster to look for a sturdy lad at the boys' orphanage. Finding no suitable teenager, they fell in love with handsome, four-year-old Len Richens. His father had sent Len there in desperation when his wife died of throat cancer, leaving him with four children and a travelling job servicing mining equipment in the Rockies. Len worked hard in Whaletown and was later joined by an older foster lad, Nat Taggert, who stayed only until he finished school, which in those days went to grade eight.

The enterprising Thompsons had numerous wealthy guests who arrived by steamship and were accommodated either in the upstairs bedrooms at the store or at the farm. Bill Robinson was able to further augment the family income when he got the job of attending to the Shark Spit light. The light ran on coal oil and could operate for two

Len Richens and Elaine Finnie plowing at Whaletown.
(Richens family photo)

days. Then the tank had to be refilled. Ed Tooker says the tanks were conical in shape to fit into the light housing. There were two tanks, so you brought home the empty one in exchange for the full one. I don't know if the keeper was required to blow out the light each morning and re-ignite it every evening or if he was allowed to let it burn for the full 48 hours. Given Ottawa's parsimonious attitude toward lighthouse keepers, it seems likely the intrepid attendant had a lot of rowing to do.

When the Thompsons died near the beginning of the Depression, Len struggled on for a while but finally sold the store and some of his land. He promptly headed for the city where his industriousness found him a steady job at Sweeney Cooperage on the north shore of False Creek, near where the old roundhouse still stands. He was delighted to find accommodation at a boarding house on Pendrell Street where his Whaletown friend Vern Borden also lived.

On a visit to Whaletown, Vern took a photograph of Elaine Finnie. When he returned to town he showed it to Len, who was impressed by the curly-haired, dainty blonde smiling out at the world. Soon he planned a holiday trip on the Union Steamship to visit the old home site. One wonders if there was some collusion, for Elaine's mother Pauline told her to meet the boat and bring Len home to dinner. Elaine had been dating Jack Schibler, a logger from Owen Bay, and mother was none too anxious to see her pretty seventeen-year-old committed to a floathouse life. When 31-year-old Len hove into view with a steady job in the city, it seemed the answer to a mother's prayer. Elaine, now in her seventies, chuckles about this as she says that Jack went on to own his own logging camp and had a home in nearby Campbell River, a cruiser, and a float plane, so it seemed her fate would not have been all that bad.

Elaine's father, Henry Finnie, had been a fireman and engineer on the railroad, but increasing deafness resulting from service at the front in World War I made him seek early retirement. In 1936 Henry and Pauline came to Whaletown, bringing young Elaine and her sister Ramona. Henry bought land and built a sturdy home on the far side of the road at the head of the lagoon, where you can see out through the entrance toward Quadra Island. The beautifully proportioned building is still in use and its current owner lovingly cares for Pauline's trees, shrubs, roses, and hedge.

Where the narrows lead to the inner lagoon you can still see some of the rocks that remain from the fish trap built by Native people long before the settlers arrived. This trap stretched out from both shores. The fishermen waited until the lagoon was full of fish. Then, as the outgoing tide was about to encourage them into deeper water, the narrow spot was blocked off with a wooden gate, effectively trapping the fish inside while the ocean drained away.

When Harry Huck sold the floating house that he'd dragged from one logging camp to another, he bought the land to the northeast of the fish trap. In 1995 his wife still lived in the little blue-and-white house with one daughter nearby. Mrs. Huck said that the trap was there when they arrived in 1940, but since the Natives weren't using it, her husband closed the gap with rocks. This allowed her and her two daughters to walk straight across to a farm on the Gorge Road where they got milk, saving them a considerable trip all around the inner lagoon. I'm not sure what this in-fill did for the spawning salmon, but they probably jumped the obstacle at high tide and carried on to their destiny.

Years earlier, Dunc Robertson had grown up on a homestead beside the lagoon. It was farther into the bay beyond the trap. He remembers dog salmon, humpies, and a few coho spawning in that little creek. One year his father got tired of the stink of decaying fish along the bank so they set to work in their gumboots, kicking the bodies into the stream. After a while the water began backing up. Dunc went downstream and found a plug of carcasses about 50 feet in length and above the level of his boot tops.

The area had been logged by Bill Barrett, who later owned the shingle mill at Carrington Bay. Barrett logged with a steam donkey before spar trees were in use. He used a 1-1/4 inch cable that was 1-1/4 miles long—the longest mainline in use at the time in B.C.—to pull logs all the way to the water.

Bill hired a relative, young Harry Middleton, to run the big steam donkey, called a yarder, with the help of a couple of other fellows. A large crew of Mongolian Chinese labourers did all the other heavy manual work. They were managed by a tiny Asian man who spoke both Chinese and English. Dunc Robertson said the labourers were all over six feet tall. Barrett started logging in 1908 and finished two years later, poorer than when he began. He seems to have had a slight case of the reverse-Midas touch.

Duncan's uncle, Charlie Allen, hired the same crew of Chinese to log in the Gorge. Charlie also bought a lot of big horses, set to work building skid roads, worked there for three years, and came out of it $5000 to the good. Apparently the Allens were regularly invited to the Chinese New Year celebration at the bunkhouse. Charlie had an East Indian mother, so perhaps he did not have the usual English problem of feeling superior to Eastern races. Whatever the reason, it seems the workers gave Charlie full measure for their dollars earned.

The roadway down to the government dock at the Gorge uses the same route as Charlie's horses did when they dragged out the logs. With the large amount of manure being produced by these "engines," the land would have benefited as well, though logging in the summer heat must have been a breathtaking experience—what with dogfish oil that was sometimes used in place of petroleum grease on the skids, and horse droppings in between. I suppose the short-lived fox farm on nearby Mary (Marina) Island, which used broken-down horses for feed, ran out of meat when donkey engines finally replaced all that live horsepower.

The three Allen brothers were homesteaders near the Gorge. Charlie was the only one right on the waterfront, near where the present marina is now located. In 1892, two of the Allens actually rowed all the way from Seattle, with a brief stop at the Fraser River in mosquito season, to Union Bay on Vancouver Island. There they learned about Cortez, where the government surveyors were busy and the land would soon be open for pre-emption. This event usually created a surge in population wherever it occurred.

*Charlie Allen's wife Jenny, with his beautiful white workhorses and a
row of the tall Chinese workers standing in the background.
(Margaret Schindler photo)*

The Allen brothers' sister, Alice, was a nurse-missionary in India,
where their father also worked. In 1894 and 1896 she visited her
brothers on Cortez, likely travelling on one of the famous Empress
ships that made fast passages across the Pacific to and from the Orient.
In India she met her future husband, David Robertson, who was just
finishing his stint with the British Army. They were married in
England and stayed there for a few years until the severe recession
in the late 1890s drove them to emigrate. They came to Vancouver
with their baby, sailing around the Horn of South America for the
exorbitant sum of eighteen dollars apiece! The Robertsons built a
house among the stumps on the south shore of False Creek, not far
from where Vancouver's city hall now stands. David Robertson was
a carpenter who worked at his trade in Vancouver and revelled in
local football, which he played with wild abandon until rheumatoid
arthritis forced him to quit work altogether. They moved to
Whaletown at the suggestion of her brothers, bought Mose Ireland's
small farm, which fronted onto the lagoon, built a larger home,
cleared more land, and raised their family. Alice and David's son
Dunc, who was 92 when I last visited him in 1998, lived at the Gorge
and was the last remaining member of that group.

According to Dunc, his Uncle Charlie Allen was a real go-getter who was very astute at reading the market. He found a ready outlet for summer produce on Savary Island during its heyday between wars. This vacation spot was abuzz with activity as residents occupied their summer homes and the hotel was full to bursting. Charlie outfitted his boat as a small store so that he and Jenny could load it up with fruit, vegetables, and eggs from local farms as well as their own. They chugged their way to the government dock at Savary where they would open up shop, then stay visiting, coming home the next day. This left their adopted daughter, Elsie, to manage the concession at their house. Earlier, in January 1914, Charlie's chicken farm was also shipping 30 dozen eggs a week to the Sing Lee Company in Powell River. This fact was duly noted in one of Charlie's many annual diaries, which were shared with me by his granddaughter Margaret Schindler of Powell River.

Charlie Allen volunteered for service in World War I and was posted to desert country. He came home in 1918 as a 50-year-old with an illness that affected his legs and a small pension to show for his bravery, but he pushed on in his efforts to earn a living in spite of the discomfort. He was appointed notary public in 1919 at the same time as his war pension commenced. He bought a boat, the *Sombrio Queen*, in Vancouver and writes in his diary about being a Fisheries Patrol Officer in 1924 and selling a one-dollar licence to Phil Lavigne of Laura Cove, among others. Fisheries patrolled over a large territory and a long season in those years, and officers went out in some ghastly weather. They were not popular with the fishermen because of the regulatory nature of their work and were nicknamed "bogey men." Both Jenny and Elsie must have worked like slaves while Charlie was away, although the huge egg production is not noted at this time. Maybe the women said, "If you go, so do the hens."

In the beginning the *Sombrio Queen* had a gas engine. In January 1919 Charlie reported in his diary: Jan. 5 "worked on [boat] all day...but only one cylinder exploding." Jan. 6 "Sent Elsie for Middleton, he warmed spark plugs up good and she started, he said the gasoline was too weak, wouldn't explode." Several times again he mutters about his gasoline-fuelled motor. According to Ed Tooker, who grew up at Coulter Bay but rowed to the Gorge to work for the Allens as a teenager, Charlie eventually installed a single-cylinder Cummins full-diesel engine. This was called an "air start" engine because you pumped a round cylinder full of air, set the flywheel so that the piston

Charlie Allen soon replaced the Sombrio Queen's *balky gas engine with a Cummins "full-diesel." (Margaret Schindler photo)*

was near the top, then released the air pressure valve. Compressed air would enter the top of the cylinder, carrying a little fuel with it and pushing the piston down. This set the flywheel to spinning so that the cylinder rose and compressed the air sufficiently to raise the internal temperature and ignite the diesel fuel. This type of manually pumped air compressor, called a Dole cylinder, was even featured for a short time in early cars like the 1915 Winton. It gave the engine a boost in starting so that the operator did not have to heave on the crank. Actually, if you were well organized and had an airtight system you could load up the cylinder during the last few turns of the engine so that you were spared the pumping job needed for starting.

The Gorge had its own lodge at the northeast end, although it was no longer active when we came in 1939. It had been built by two speculators, Cavanaugh and Jones, who scouted out likely spots, cleared land, put up buildings, and then sold them to hopeful buyers, in this case, Tena Corneille. Tena had visited nearby Mary (Marina) Island in 1919 with her husband, who was on sick leave from the Brackman-Kerr Feed Company office in Vancouver. They rented a house at Chamadaska village and Tena made many friends in the area. Unfortunately, Mr. Corneille died of tuberculosis of the bone while on Mary Island. Tena had to wait three days with the body before the Union Steamship arrived to ferry them to Vancouver and eventually to Victoria where her husband wanted to be buried.

Tena's husband had adequate life insurance but had never changed the beneficiary from his mother to his wife. He had assured Tena that his mother would do "the right thing." She did...for herself, rejecting her daughter-in-law's claim and leaving Tena with three children aged five to twelve, a house in Kerrisdale, and cooking as

The Wacondah *ferried people to the Gorge Harbour Lodge from Manson's Landing. Here Alan Georgeson, Tena Corneille, Mabelle Corneille, and Edith Munday are standing on the dock, with Bobby and Bill Ballantyne seated and G.G. Ballantyne in the boat.*
(Bobby Ballantyne photo)

her only marketable skill. Tena struggled on in Vancouver, selling baking and cooking lunches for some of the teachers at the local school while her children finished their education. Then she sold out, got help from her sister, and bought the lodge at the Gorge for $6000 in 1929.

By this time Tena's son Fred was 22 and had a job on the coastal steamships. Her daughters, Mabelle, 19, and Bobby, 15, helped around the lodge. Tena Corneille, at four-foot-ten, set to work and made it into a thriving enterprise with a big marquee tent to house large family groups, three smaller tents for sleeping, and five bedrooms in the main building, which also had a lounge for rainy day activities. With her contacts in Kerrisdale and through her husband's friends she went on to house a steady stream of visitors. They happily paid $6.65 for a round-trip ticket from Vancouver to visit the Lodge. In later years this tiny, indefatigable woman said that the move to the Gorge was the best thing she ever did.

The 15-and-under race is about to begin at the Gorge Annual Regatta, with Bobby Corneille already in the water. (Bobby Ballantyne photo)

Bobby (Corneille) Ballantyne, who lives in Campbell River, remembers there was lots of work to do to keep the lodge running. Laundry was done in a washer with a wooden tub and a big lever on the side that you pushed and pulled. The clothes were squeezed between rubber rollers, turned by a big hand crank, to extract the water, then rinsed, wrung, and rinsed again before being squashed dry and hung out on clotheslines. No handy laundromats in those days, but oh, clean, sunbaked clothes and sheets smelled wonderful! Bobby and Mabelle also smoothed and rolled the clay tennis courts by four in the morning, cut the grass with a hand mower, and generally maintained the place, with Bobby doing all the carpentry work.

Mabelle ran their boat, *Wacondah*, ferrying passengers and baggage to and fro from Manson's Landing and Whaletown, as well as hauling the shipments of groceries that came in from Woodward's store in Vancouver. The yacht was about 28 feet long with a rounded stern and covered cockpit that could be made weatherproof by rolling down canvas side-curtains. There was a bench around the inside of the transom, seats inside, and a little toilet right forward, but no galley. After the original engine expired it was replaced with a Little Wonder, which had formerly been used by loggers to pump water for fighting forest fires This little plant had one cylinder that featured an automatic intake valve. It looked a bit like an Easthope but put out a scant four horsepower. To keep weight to a minimum for firefighters, most of the metal was aluminum, except for the flywheel, crankshaft, and cylinder.

In order to gain confidence in running it, Mabelle spent time with Harry Middleton to learn about engines. According to Frank Tooker, whenever it wouldn't start Mabelle would take the motor apart. Frank said the problem was usually that it was flooded with too much gas, and a little patient waiting would have done the trick. Bobby added that when Mabelle had it apart, you resorted to using the big sweep oars while standing facing forward in the cockpit. They took advantage of the currents through the Gorge when they could. By the time she was 17, Bobby was running the boat herself.

Every summer Tena Corneille put on a big regatta with water and land sports, a refreshment table, and a dance in the evening. Ed Tooker remembered winning the rowboat races four consecutive summers because rowing was essential to his livelihood as a teenager. The feature event was a swimming race between Rankin Robertson and his niece, Winnifred. The race was won, often as not, by the girl.

When we came into the Gorge that summer, we tied up at Charlie Allen's dock. While Mother and Dad visited, my brother and I took the rowboat and cruised slowly along the shore, spearing Dungeness crabs with a trident fastened to the end of a long pole. There are so few of these delicacies around today that tridents are no longer legal; one has to use traps into which the crab must volunteer to climb. But in those early days we used whatever worked. The water was crystal clear but it took George a while to get the refraction worked out so that he could hit the crabs and not the stones. Nobody had thought of goggles and snorkels in those days. It was my first taste of crab and I wasn't all that impressed, probably because my mother insisted on cooking all seafood to death.

Next morning we motored out through the narrow defile of the entrance, slowing to take pictures of the Native rock paintings on the steep cliffs. They were lit by the early light and were still clear and decipherable. We passed Ned Breeze's place, which was nestled into the left-hand side of the opening. Ned was trained as a druggist but had rowed to Cortez Island with his wife many years earlier. He had probably come into a modest inheritance that allowed him to abandon his career and follow his dream west. When the local people became ill he'd mix a potion for them to use, so it seems he did not entirely abandon his calling.

After his wife and daughter died, he stayed on at their home site for many years. Ed Tooker came over from Coulter Bay as a teenager to cut firewood for Ned, who told him about his early life. One day when Ned was almost 80 he fell while trying to spread hot tar on his roof, so he wisely hired Ed to finish the job. He felt responsible for the protection of the Indian burial caves under the cliff edge on his property, but try as he might he could not prevent souvenir hunters from raiding them and they were all but stripped bare. When I saw the caves years later they mesmerized me, sheltered as they were by huge maple trees that carpeted the floors with golden leaves. Besides the caves, Ned cherished the deer that were so tame he fed them by hand.

After he died, his property was divided among his nieces and nephews of the FitzJames family. Their father had been the CEO of a Vancouver firm that manufactured all the wooden pipe that was used to carry water to canneries and mills up and down the B.C. coast. (You can still see a section of this pipe lying at Refuge Cove near the stream at the back of the store.) This very durable pipe was made of curved and jointed strips of black preservative-coated cedar and held together with a continuous binding of metal coil.

Mrs. FitzJames was a Shaw and was related to George Bernard Shaw, so she was likely the source of most of Ned's library. Charlie Allen's granddaughters said they loved to row out to visit Ned because he always welcomed them and shared his collection of *National Geographic* magazines. Every Christmas, Elsie (Allen) Beattie had Ned come over for dinner along with three other single old-timers who lived in the Gorge area. Ned always had thoughtful presents for Elsie's children. He also worked out a signalling system with a lonely old bachelor called Harry Bowerman who lived across from him on the shores of Mary Island at the old fox farm. When either household failed to display a flag up a pole, Harry or Ned knew the other was trouble and would row over to investigate and see what help was needed.

The centre of activity on Mary Island was around the old Native village site at Chamadaska, just opposite Manson's Landing. In the heyday of white settlement there was even a Chamadaska Post Office, a government dock for the Union Steamships, and sufficient children for a school. It is sad that more of the original Native names were not retained on our coast. Chamadaska Island had at least two other large Native settlements at one time. There was one near a deep cut-bank

The fox farm that prospered for a while at Chamadaska on Mary Island. After the farm was abandoned it became a source for chicken-run wire that stayed rust free for years. (Margaret Schindler photo)

of a stream about opposite Paukeneum. Another was in a bay on the southwest side of the island just past the huge reef. On a rock in front of this village site there is a petroglyph of two interlocking faces wearing frightening expressions.

A man by the name of Marlatt built a handsome two-storey log house on the side of the island that faces Heriot Bay. My dad said the fireplace was so large you could practically stand up in it. According to reports, the house was filled with high-quality hardwood furniture and eventually was nicely landscaped. There was even a large monkey puzzle tree in the garden. Mr. Marlatt re-named the island after his mother, Mary, which was not that different from Captain Vancouver's choice of Marina.

The family arrived in June 1907 and Mr. Marlatt set to work removing the fine virgin timber on the island. Since they were using steam donkeys to drag the logs out and selling to a very picky market, they took only the finest, straightest, number one timber, leaving lots for later workers to gather.

Marlatt hired young Harry Middleton to run a steam donkey. One day there was a nasty accident in which a logger was struck across the forehead by a cable that suddenly leapt free from a hang-up. The cable sliced open his forehead and lay the scalp back parallel with his ears. The whistle punk frantically tootled for the donkey to release the cable, and Harry came running in answer to the shouts. He picked off the worst of the pine needles and hauled the scalp back over the exposed bone, then had the crew rip the man's shirt into a wide bandage so that he could bind the tear into place.

When the local nurse saw the mess she wanted to pull off the bandage and clean the area, but Harry shouted, "You leave that right

Chamadaska dock on Mary Island, just opposite Manson's Landing. In later years the whole dock was swept away during a winter gale.
(Campbell River Museum photo)

alone." They revved up the boat engine and hurried the man to the doctor. He said that Harry had done the best thing and then simply stitched up the wound as it was. Years later, when he was walking down Granville Street in Vancouver, Harry was stopped by a fellow who said, "I guess you don't remember me." When Harry seemed puzzled the man pulled off his cap and raised the hair off his forehead. He said that the wound had healed beautifully but that pine needles continued to erupt through the scalp for a while after the accident.

Another young man who joined the crew in 1911 as steam donkey engineer was Hank Herrewig. He had come from Wisconsin, as did many people. Perhaps the news of huge trees lured the loggers here, or maybe Wisconsin had an excellent travel agent. It wasn't long before Hank discovered Hazel Manson, one of the attractive daughters of Michael and Jane Manson.

Hank and Hazel were married and he continued working at different logging camps as a steam donkey engineer. They eventually took up residence in the house that my grandparents had rented when they first arrived on the scene. Hazel inherited that "Big House" at the same time as her sister Flo got the property at Gunflint Lake. The Herrewigs turned the front parlour of the Big House into a store.

Erskine *at Manson's dock with the wharf shed not yet built.*
(Mike Herrewig photo)

In 1921 Hank and Hazel's son Mike was enrolled in the school at Manson's Landing, where the teacher was none other than my father, 24-year-old George Griffin.

Hank had a large boat, the *Erskine*, which he anchored outside the mouth of the lagoon. He had acquired this distinctive boat from the rumrunning trade. The large craft had outlived its usefulness for that purpose because it was so well known—or nefarious—that it could not stick its nose out of Vancouver Harbour without being nabbed by the police. The owner of the rumrunner accepted in exchange the small cruiser *Wonewoc*, which Hank had built himself. Once he got his notorious boat safely away from the city, Hank put it to work as a general freight boat and as a fish buyer serving the handtrollers and small gas boats that worked the area.

During winter storms, Hank kept his boat inside the Manson Lagoon, as do many today. It takes a fairly high ingoing tide and local knowledge to get past the shallows, but once within there is a fine pool of deep, sheltered water in which to drop your anchor. Etta Byers says that the name Clytosin, which the spit of land was first called, means "water on both sides."

By this time, activity on Mary Island, just opposite Manson's, was winding down. One of Mr. Marlatt's sons had gone into training as a medical doctor and worked for a time with the Columbia Coast Mission, then at Texada Island, before setting up a practice in Powell

River in 1920. Another son became a dentist. Ed Tooker, who now lives at Westview, speaks fondly of the Dr. Marlatt who worked on their teeth.

When we cruised past Mary Island that summer in 1939 there was no evidence of the dock that had seen so many comings and goings in those early days. The old fox farm was deserted and tumbled down, but it still supplied local people with high-quality galvanized chicken wire that showed not a sign of rust. With no bays to provide safe harbours for small boats and no vast amount of sandy beaches like Savary boasted, the island had few attractions once the timber was gone.

We continued on around the island toward Reef (Sutil) Point, which was not connected to Manson's Landing and the rest of Cortez Island by land until John Lambert built a trail after arriving on the island in 1908. John was a widower who settled in this remote area with his eldest son Tom. He kept a simple diary in which he recorded the weather and his activities, including the days he worked on building a trail from his place overlooking the reef to meet the wagon trail that led to Manson's place. He wanted a land route to the trading post so they did not have to make the trip by water.

In those early days, Lambert noted in his dairy that in January 1909 he got a cheque for $46.88 for his work on the trail and sent it downtown with John Manson. Downtown could have been Comox, where John rowed his meat for sale, or Vancouver, anywhere there was a bank to cash it.

Lambert worked hard trying to earn a living. Not only did he continue with the trail, but he also tried raising chickens, hatching his own chicks in a brooder. To feed his growing flock he had to row to the trading post for wheat and carry it up from the boat on his back. He notes that on August 8 he arranged for someone called Claude to look after his chickens while he went to fall trees for the Newman camp. He worked at the camp wherever he was needed until October 18, for which he earned the princely sum of $168.

John Lambert and his neighbour, Mr. Padgett, organized a local committee for the Conservative Party, which had its first meeting in the schoolhouse near Clytosin on October 26, 1909. The Padgetts and the Lamberts worked to get Michael Manson elected to the legislature in Victoria.

Lambert also notes in his diary the times he was a dinner guest of the Padgetts. The Padgett place was just at the end of the current

Stuart, Gertie, and Russell Lambert at Tom's homestead above Reef Point. This is the same house later occupied in the summer by George and Nat Hodson when they fished for salmon.

road in Smelt Bay, next to where the park and government campsite are now located. Their old log barn stood there for years and was photographed and included in many paintings. If you have access to a copy of Bill Wolferstan's *Desolation Sound Cruising Guide*, the rusted roof of the barn is very noticeable in the aerial photograph of Smelt Bay. Native people chose this location centuries earlier for a permanent winter home. The huge trenches, variously called longhouse pits or defence earthworks, are still visible to mark their presence. According to Lester Peterson in his book on the Sechelt People, warlike raids among lower coast tribes were a result of the disruption of balance caused by the arrival of white traders, so I like to think of these hollows as home sites of an earlier day rather than the signs of conflict.

Padgetts kept a herd of goats. They eventually moved first to Texas Island and later to Myrtle Point, south of Powell River, where goat farming stood a chance of supporting a family. When they left they gave some of their goats to the Lamberts. In 1917, when Henry Byers was running a logging show near their farm, his group built a big wood-and-rock breakwater to protect their booming grounds in this exposed place. One day he was bending over greasing skids when he heard a shout, "Watch out, Henry!" He leaped to one side just in time to avoid being bunted down by the Lambert billy goat. Another time he was not so lucky. He was out on a boomstick bending over, with the goat the farthest thing from his mind, when he was struck from behind and dumped in the salt chuck by the goat that thought it was a logger.

Earlier, in 1913, Tom Lambert had married Gertie Ripple, who came to Cortez from Minnesota as a young girl. Her mother moved to the island to marry Augustus Tiber. The new Mrs. Tiber would have been admirably prepared for the rough life on Cortez, for it seems electricity had not yet arrived in Minnesota either. Gertie attended the one-room log school with two sets of Manson twins. After their wedding in Vancouver, Gertie and Tom came to live in the house that he and his dad built at Reef Point. According to Gertie, her first chore upon arrival was to do up a huge sink full of dirty dishes that awaited her. I guess John ran out of steam in preparing a reception for the newlyweds; small wonder with all the work involved in homesteading. It was with delight that I read in her unpublished life story, lent to me by Nellie Jeffery, that her children had my dad, George Griffin, as their teacher. In the picture of the Manson School pupils of 1921 you can find Stuart Lambert along with my younger uncles and aunts, with my dad in the back row.

Over the years many people have lived in the house Lambert built for his son and have enjoyed fruit from the Lamberts' varied orchard. My brother camped there with Nat Hodson when they rowboat fished off the reef. By that time the house had been long abandoned. Today a Manson descendent, Bruce Ellingsen, and his delightful wife Jinny live on the farm, which they have named Reef Point. You can buy eggs laid by Jinny's chickens at the Cortez Island Market near the community hall.

My father boarded for a time at the Cullen place, which had originally belonged to the Padgetts. Both Dad and my Aunt Alice remember Mrs. Cullen admonishing them not to chew too much meat off the chicken bones because she needed them to make soup for the next meal. Alice also remembers the geese on the farm. They were fantastic "watchdogs" that challenged her each time she came to play with Mimi. Woe betide the unexpected visitor who wasn't met at the gate by one of the family.

Mrs. Cullen's son, Hartley, was an outstanding needleworker. Not only did he knit, embroider, and sew, but he also tailored from scratch. Alice particularly remembers the beautiful wedding dress he made for his sister. Hartley went on to become a bank manager, but his first love was needlework. What a pity he didn't live in a metropolis where he could have become couturier to the rich. It is likely that in pioneer B.C. he received little understanding, for the frontier mentality dissuaded most young men from engaging in any of the gentle arts.

Near the Cullens lived the O'Donnells, who are also mentioned in Lambert's diary. Alice said that Mrs. O'Donnell had a glorious head of white hair that she kept from yellowing in the sun by rinsing it in laundry bluing. Every conscientious housewife of the day kept a little block of Ricketts bluing to add to the final rinse so that her white clothing would look frosty white instead of "tattle-tale grey."

Mr. O'Donnell had established a nursery where most local settlers came to get the stock of fruit trees, shrubs, and berry bushes they needed to meet the requirements of pre-empting. When I heard about this, I knew that my grandfather had arrived too late, because the settlers already had a reliable nursery. Cap Smith of Seaford, for one, had come to O'Donnell in the early years to get stock to establish his varied orchard, which included a mulberry bush. When I asked Nellie Jeffery about this ancient berry she said that it was almost a little tree in shape, with fruit that was white and as sweet as honey. They didn't attempt to make jam from it, however, as they had so many other colourful fruit like gooseberries, currants, and raspberries from which they could make preserves.

Mr. O'Donnell became very ill, possibly with prostate cancer. He travelled to Vancouver to seek help and was sent back home to die. He boarded the Union Steamship in the city, but when it arrived at Manson's Landing he was nowhere to be found.

We did not stop at Smelt Bay the summer that we returned from our search for a logger. Dad tended to be hyper-cautious about anchoring in exposed areas, so we continued out around the reef on our way back to Blind Creek.

There is a shortcut through the big spread of rocks off Reef Point. My brother took me through it on the *Wag*. I hung nervously over the bow watching for rocks while he casually gutted salmon in the stern. At a sufficiently high tide you line up a point on Mary Island with a big tree on Hernando and keep an eye over the side in case of sideways drift from the current. At low tide you can see the pass among the boulders on the sands but you can't use it.

Anchored floating buoys like the one at Reef Point were equipped with both a bell, that was struck by clappers as the buoy rocked with the waves, and a light that shone day and night. I asked Mike Herrewig how the light was powered, as solar batteries had not yet been invented and coal oil lamps would have been the very devil to maintain in such an exposed place. He said that the lamp consisted of a reservoir in which carbide crystals were stored. A timed drip of water on the carbide produced a gas that was ignited by a small pilot light, providing a burst of flame that flared up, then went out as the gas was consumed. The frequency of the drip could be controlled so that the light flashed in a pre-set sequence, allowing cartographers to indicate on the charts the number of seconds between flashes for each buoy. The buoys needed regular maintenance, and misfires did occur, but the presence of the bell buoy saved many a boat from disaster as it navigated around this treacherous reef.

From the buoy we could see, to the southwest, the barren islet called Mitlenatch (the German word for midnight). At the turn of the century Maggie and John Manson lived in a little house on this barren rock. John had brought Maggie, his childhood sweetheart, from the Shetland Islands after they married, but she was so homesick that he decided to live right on Mitlenatch where he pastured his sheep so that she would not feel so lonely. John was often away, rowing to Comox to sell his mutton to the Cumberland miners or doing his duty as watchman for the Hastings Mill logging sites in the area. This left Maggie alone on Mitlenatch with two small children and expecting the next. Sometimes a canoeload of Natives would stop to visit. She couldn't speak their language, but she offered them food, which they ate as they squatted around outside. No wonder she felt unhappy, as she had probably read the usual American Wild

"Uncle" John Manson with Bud Turner (an autistic boy who boarded with them) atop bales of wool from the Mitlenatch sheep. (May Ellingsen photo)

*Maggie Manson lived in the cabin
on Mitlenatch when her babies were small.*

West tales about scalping. Later John moved the family to a large parcel of land on Cortez that overlooked Hernando Island. There they lived out their lives, with John saying that as long as he could till the land and grow his potatoes, he was happy.

In the late 1920s my Aunt Alice went with "Uncle" John and Irene Turner to visit Mitlenatch when John was shearing his sheep. Irene, who became Alice's good friend, spent her holidays at the Manson house, visiting with her brother Bud, an autistic child who boarded year-round at the household. Alice said that they stayed in the little shelter John had erected, picked wild flowers, studied the cactus plants, watched nesting birds, and learned how to gather seagull eggs to cook for breakfast. When the sky began to cloud over, John said it was a "masatchee" sky (the Native word for stormy or bad) and he hurried them into the rowboat and set out for home.

We did not go to Mitlenatch on our trip but swung the *Loumar's* bow around the buoy, glided past John Manson's Cortez Island farm, past the "Jap" ranch, around the top of the Twin Islands, past Ashford Bay, and back into Blind Creek.

12 ROWBOAT FISHING, DOGFISHING, AND OTHER FUN!

When my family's house was built in 1940, it was occupied all winter. Dad had been approached by a trio of rowboat fishermen who were later dubbed the Three Musketeers, probably in reference to their usual method of acquiring meat. They were broke and needed a place to spend the winter, so when we left at the end of summer they moved in. This arrangement helped Dad fulfill the requirement for pre-emption that the house be lived in year-round within the first five years.

During the Depression, welfare as we know it did not exist. To get a meagre bit of support from the government you had to declare yourself an indigent, which carried a real social stigma that prevented many people from accepting help. One man with small children humbly asked for assistance. Because he lived on the land he was sent a rake, shovel, and some seeds, period, and that was in December. Around Cortez and the other islands, some men lived along the shoreline in lean-to shelters while they rowboat fished to make a bare living. There were about 40 such dwellings along the end of Cape Mudge that were occupied during the season by these hardy souls. In spring and fall they went after cod or the large salmon that is variously called spring, silver, or king. The smaller salmon—coho (blueback), sockeye, chum (dog salmon), or pink—all arrive in what are known as runs that occur from June until early fall, when fishing becomes a frenzy.

It must have been a chilly winter in our cottage if the fireplace facing was any indication. It was stained with soot to the ceiling. Later on we found that the southeast winter winds came over the bluff behind the house and roared straight down the flue.

Georgie and Nat in Blind Creek, loaded with gear for squatting in the Lambert cabin while rowboat fishing off Reef Point.

When we came back to Blind Creek in the summer, only one musketeer, Nat Hodson, remained. As he planned to fish off Reef Point that year, he invited my brother George to join him. They rowed their boats, loaded with camping gear, all the way around to the reef, made a skidway of peeled cedar poles through the boulders, and set up housekeeping in the deserted Lambert homestead on top of the bluff. For refrigeration they hung their perishables down the well. These included a few pitlamped deer and, I suspect, the odd small sheep from John Manson's flock on Mitlenatch Island.

The term "pitlamp" originated with the lamps miners fastened on their caps so that they could work underground. In island terms it meant going out after dark when the deer were feeding and shining a light in their eyes. This seemed to mesmerize the animal long enough for a hunter to line up his gun and get in a shot before it whirled and leaped away into the brush. For people short of meat and plagued by deer eating their hard-won crop of vegetables, any method that got results would do. Rowboat fishermen made use of this ready source of meat, as well as fish.

George and Nat fished together for two years, with George graduating to a carvel-built, double-ended rowboat and then to a sailboat that Dad built for us and that George powered with a washing machine motor. I graduated first to our old clinker-built rowboat and then to the double-ender. When Nat moved on, George and I fished as a team, though I lacked his total dedication.

The equipment needed to catch fish was simple, probably because they were so plentiful. For a reel I needed a flat piece of

Georgie in the clinker-built rowboat with some of his hand-trolled fish caught in Baker Pass, 1940.

wood, notched at either end. I rolled a length of dark-green linen cod line onto this. We had made the weights the winter before by melting lead in a can over a blowtorch and pouring it into wooden moulds, into which we inserted the necessary wire ends. At the end of the cod line was a brass swivel onto which I fastened what was called a flasher. These were usually homemade and were a rectangular shape about the size of a man's shoe, bent up at one end and down at the other. Each fisherman had his or her own private style of cutting and bending these lures. Taking a fine piece of stainless steel wire, I slipped it through another brass swivel on the trailing end of the flasher. By wrapping the short end of this wire snugly around the shaft of the main piece and then wiggling it vigorously back and forth until it snapped off, I was left with a strong barbless connection. I went through this whole process again to fasten on the blue-grey metal hook, about two-and-a-half inches long and guaranteed to rust. Through the eye of the hook I threaded a piece of extra fine wire, almost as thin as a human hair, so that I could tie my herring onto the hook.

Now all I needed was a live herring. They were available in abundance. During the winter we prepared a thin slat of edge-grain fir about three-and-a-half inches wide and ten feet long. Along one edge near the end we carefully inserted steel pins, two-and-a-half inches long, setting them in snugly about half an inch apart for about three feet. (If you couldn't afford steel pins you made do with cut sections of Staybrite leader wire.) When finished, the end result looked not unlike a giant's short-toothed comb, but it was known as a herring rake and was likely nothing new to the Native people of the area. I tucked this into the bow of my boat, giving it a decidedly narwhal appearance, and then set out to find a school of bait, which could be needlefish or various sizes of herring.

I can think of nothing more primal than raking herring. I would watch the surface of the water for the telltale circles, bubbles, and swirls the small fish made while they nibbled on plankton. Then I would row toward this disturbance, oh, so quietly, carefully shipping my oars as I came near. Ever so gently I would crawl forward to the bow, kneel with the rake in my hands, use it as a paddle, and carefully shake off the drips before I stretched it out over the busy school of fish. Like a heron I would reach the business end forward slowly and cautiously. When it seemed just the right time I would swish the rake edgewise through the school in one continuous movement, carrying it back and up over the after end of my boat, twisting my wrist so the teeth pointed downwards, and shaking the silver catch loose into the bilge. A quick scramble and the herring were swimming in my live bait tank. I would wait a few moments and then go through the routine again when the fish seemed to collectively feel they were safe and resumed cruising in a group. The still, quiet concentration of this slow routine made me lose my sense of time as I peered down into the rich blue, green, silver, and violet moving rays of light in the clear, deep water. Is it today or was it 200 years ago?

I became so skilled at finding schools of these tiny fish that it almost seemed psychic. I got so that I could actually smell their presence, although I was afraid to tell anyone for fear of ridicule. A few summers ago, when I was motoring in my sailboat over glassy smooth water between Sointula and Port Hardy, I clearly detected the same smell. I slowed down and caught a feeding coho amid swirls of tiny herring. It was then that I decided to share this intuition with a fisheries officer. He said researchers had discovered that schools of bait fish emit a gas that bubbles to the surface, enabling predators like seagulls to find their food source even in the roughest sea conditions. Maybe the next exotic, expensive gear the fishermen will all need to buy will be a sniff-o-meter. Or maybe they will go back to purist rowboat fishing with nothing clouding their senses.

In those faraway days, when I had raked the bait we both needed, I was ready to fish. I slipped the hook through the herring's mouth, down through the gut, and out at the vent. (It sounds like a method of medieval torture when I put it into print.) To hold the bait on the hook I wound the hair-like wire around just behind the gills. Then I fed out my line until the flasher was about 30 feet behind my boat, looped the soft cod line behind my right calf, and commenced to row. Rowing allowed me to vary the trolling speed and change direction easily so that my wounded herring looked exactly like what it was…a crippled fish, an irresistible lure to a hungry salmon.

As I approached a school of herring I would take a strong pull on my oars and let my gear sink as the boat slowed. As I glided along I would see the sheen of the salmon backs or glimpse the flash of silver bellies as they twisted to snap at their breakfast. Since both the feed and the salmon were near the surface, I simply had to drag my shining bait erratically beneath an active school of herring. I could feel a strike immediately by the tweak on my leg. I would ship the oars and pull in the line with no fooling around playing the fish. A heave up over the side of the boat with my fingers curled around the trailing edge of the flasher, a quick whack with my fish bonker, and I rebaited, ready for the next one.

I loved that carvel-planked, fifteen-foot double-ender. This treasure of a rowboat was bought with the money George earned in the first summer with Nat. A teacher friend, Lea Smith from Hornby Island, built it in his basement in Vancouver, planking it smoothly in half-inch cedar. Near the stern there was a live-bait well, just where you could comfortably brace your feet for pulling on the oars. The salt water ran in and out of this well through two little holes. A mesh of wires set into the opening prevented all but the smallest herring from escaping. Behind the well was the fish hold where you put your catch under a wet burlap sack.

Lea made a pair of long oars that had a hollow drilled in the handle. We poured molten lead into this hollow so that the outer ends had no weight to them. The oars were spoon shaped, with a thin brass capping strip in case we inadvertently struck them on the beach. They crossed over each other as they came through the middle of a pull, but when I leaned forward and dipped them into the water, then drew my hands toward me, the boat slid along for more than the length of the hull. To keep the rowlocks from rattling, each hole was oversized so I could wrap a thin piece of leather around the pin and keep it lubricated with Vaseline. If my shins got too sunburned I could smear a little of this same product on them to keep toilet paper glued there as a shield.

George made a hammock device that raised the rower just off the wooden seat. It consisted of the bottom and ends of a rectangular wooden box. Along the top edge of each end he drilled holes through which he threaded cod line back and forth to make a webbing. When I put this on the thwart with a small cotton pad beneath my bottom, I could row all day without getting blisters on my working end.

At the end of each fishing day we pulled this light craft up on the dock that my dad had anchored in our bay. We washed out the inside with salt water, wiping away the slime and scales of the day, then dried it all over with a cloth and turned it upside down for the night to await another day. In those summers I often left Blind Creek before dawn, caught a tow outside the harbour around to Ashford Bay, rowed and fished my way to Reef Point, fished until lunch time, took a midday nap with a kelp head looped through the oarlock to act as an anchor while I curled up in the bow, then fished again until it was time to be towed over to the fish-buying scow that was anchored in a small bight called Garden Bay, just down from the log house on Twin Islands. I believe I got less than six cents a pound for bluebacks. That was also the year I was the first and only female member of the Kitsilano High School weightlifting club, where Doug Hepburn trained before he went on to win a gold medal at the Olympics.

When fishing was particularly good, George set up housekeeping in one of the old houses that sat abandoned at Stag Bay on Hernando Island. Since these had stood empty for many years, the floors were virtually rotted out in the back rooms, but the front rooms were habitable as long as you put your bed under a piece of intact roof. These had been well-built cottages made of sawn lumber, not a bit like the fairly primitive cabins usually found upcoast. This group of settlers had spent money and planned on staying a long time. They had obviously swallowed the publicity about making their fortune on free land, as many settlers did.

George built a primitive stove, using scraps of abandoned ones, and set it on a bed of rocks and sand with the chimney going out a window hole. He anchored his power skiff in the bay and kept the

Manson house at Stag Bay, Hernando Island, is still in use today. The inset shows Wilf Manson wearing his favourite logging hat before hardhats were in use. (Dorothy MacDougal photo)

rowboat tied there during the daytime. If a big northwest wind seemed imminent he anchored in Dog Bay to the south. The fish-buying scow with store was in sight across Baker Pass, so he had an easy trip to get there.

I spent a couple of nights with him on Hernando. There was no glass in the windows, and the breezes kept the air fresh. The floor was fragile in places so you trod with care, and the back rooms certainly smelled ratty, but at least there was a sort of roof over your head and you had a good view of the bay, the sunsets, and your anchored boat. George had found old bedsprings, which he padded with newspapers in lieu of a mattress. As I had never camped out before I did not know that you must put as much under you as over you if you plan to keep warm. I had only brought along my quilt from the cabin, where I had a mattress under me. On Hernando I shivered all night and assumed my brave brother must put up with such discomfort because he was hardier than I was. On the second night I rolled myself up in the covers.

There was a large, brown, carpenter-built house in the curve of Stag Bay. It had been built in 1928 for Wilf Manson, the only surviving son of Michael and Jane. The fish buyer and his wife who ran the scow tied in by the Twin Islands lived there in the off-season, acting

Small fishboats found shelter at Mitlenatch
during summer runs of salmon. (Helen Anderson photo)

as caretakers. We went to visit one day. Coming from a conventional, tidy house I was not prepared for the total disarray that met my eyes as we stepped through the door. There were old newspapers and magazines piled waist high alongside crates and boxes full of junk. A narrow pathway led to the table. Here there were two clear places at either end where you could fit in dinner plates if you wriggled them a bit. The oilcloth table covering was grey, but if you looked carefully you could see the flower pattern under the film of dirt. The rest of the table was littered with open jam pots, cups with antique coffee dried up in the bottom, and scraps of food of unknown origin. A crowd of bluebottle flies buzzed around them. I'm afraid I just stood there bug-eyed while my brother conducted the business for which we'd come. I was terrified we'd be offered something to eat.

Later that summer my brother bought pork chops at the scow and proudly carried them home for dinner. We were always short of fresh meat, so my mother happily opened the package only to gasp in horror; the food was alive with maggots. George's face fell at the sight as this purchase had been made with his hard-earned fishing dollars. When she saw his expression Mother assured him everything would be fine and proceeded to wash the chops. I tried my best to eat them after she had cooked them to leather, but I couldn't. He never again bought anything from that source. Yet the rowboat fishermen had no choice because the other scows were as far away as Bliss Landing or Refuge Cove.

As World War II got into full swing there was an urgent demand for dogfish livers. We were told they were used to manufacture vitamin A and D to help keep our airmen keen of sight. What we were not told is that dogfish liver oil was the best lubricant that could be used at sea to keep gun mounts swivelling and to lubricate anything else that salt water gummed up. (Any West Coast Native person could have told them that!) Sometimes I think the U-boat captains only had to open their turrets and sniff if they wanted to track down allied warships. Can you imagine the downwind aroma in the warmer climes?

At any rate, many fishermen moved from the none-too-profitable salmon fishery to dogfishing. As I recall, the bay next to the red granite one outside Blind Creek was where the fishermen congregated to strip and sell their catch. Although it was called Windy Bay, it should have had a more descriptive title at the time, although that would depend on what kind of wind you meant.

Anyone who has trolled for salmon has caught a dogfish at least once. The response is usually one of disgust because we have not learned to use this mini-shark as the English fishmongers have. If the fish is skinned immediately upon being caught, or if the flesh is soaked in vinegar or lemon juice, you cannot tell the difference between it and cod. Without these precautions the meat takes on the stench of ammonia or of old, wet, cloth diapers.

Dogfish prefer aromatic bait, slow speed, and deep trolling as they have to roll over to get the food into their mouth. With their long, shark-like nose and underslung jaw they are incapable of snatching at fast-moving lures. When you hook a dogfish it tends to sound, or head for the bottom, just as a big spring salmon does. But unlike a salmon it stays down there and sulks. When you finally drag it up to the surface it looks at you balefully until you pull it free from its element. Then it thrashes about trying to rake you with a nasty spike that protrudes just in front of its dorsal fin. It keeps on writhing and twisting until you finally manage to bash it senseless; not an easy task under the circumstances.

The only part of the fish used by the war effort was the liver. Fishermen would pack the livers in tall, square, metal tins with round lids that fit snugly down on top—though after a few days you got to feel that this lid was not snug enough. Each metal container held 40 pounds, and at the height of the fishery the price went to four dollars a pound. Fish buyers inspected the full tins by inserting a kind of hypodermic needle down into the container to take a sample of the contents. This sample was processed at labs owned by some of the large fishing companies, with the results of the test determining whether the fisher would be paid for his or her work. The independent fishermen felt at a disadvantage among the company boats, possibly for good reason.

Wilf Manson used the Erskine *to pick up fish from the rowboats and transfer the catch to the scow. (Dorothy MacDougal photo)*

My Uncle Dick Finnie joined in this lucrative fishery, and Rod was his deckhand. They caught most of their fish, including a few sharks, in Baker Pass. Uncle Dick said that large female dogfish had the finest livers of all.

Two young women whom I admired greatly, Dorothy Manson and her friend Dorcas Essen, also joined the dogfishery. They used the *Scotia*, a small troller that Dorothy's dad, Wilf, used for a year before he realized that what he really needed was a large boat to pick up the fishermen's catch on site. Then he bought the *Erskine* from Hank Herrewig. The two girls fished salmon during the day and jigged for dogfish in the evening off the side of the fish-buyer's barge, which was anchored at that time in Stag Bay in front of Dorothy's house on Hernando Island. It was usual for the handtrollers to gut fish right on the barge, and the dogfish quickly located this gourmet dining spot. Dorothy said she rigged up a pole to catch the dogfish and put a bell on the line so that she could stop for dinner and still know when she had a fish.

Dorothy had lived on the island until she was seven, when she left to spend winters going to school in the Kitsilano area of Vancouver where she stayed with her maternal grandmother. In the summers she'd come back up the coast. Dorothy was the oldest child in her family and had spent considerable time on boats with her dad, so

Eighteen-year-old Dorothy Manson fishing from the Scotia
off Twin Islands. (Dorothy MacDougal photo)

she had a good marine background before she took over the *Scotia*. She told me that she ran the fishboat all by herself the first year, when she was seventeen, but was really glad when her friend Dorcas joined her as a deckhand for the next two summers. She said that they enjoyed themselves immensely and became brave enough to take the high-tide shortcut across the reef on their way to Manson's Landing. Once they even caught a huge skate off the end of the steamer dock there and had a tough time hauling it up past the pilings. The young people often congregated at the wharf in the evening to socialize. This explains why Dorothy and Dorcas were returning home to Hernando late one velvety dark night, navigating around the reef more by instinct than anything else, when they abruptly came upon an unlighted tug towing a log boom. It was only luck that prevented them running right up high and dry on the logs.

When my brother and I were fishing we regularly saw the two young women hauling lines as they went by. Sometimes George gave me control of the *Wag* while he took the double-ender in among the kelp heads in search of big spring salmon. Once I repaid his habit of overestimating my ability by losing the leads on Centre Rock, a hidden hazard that lurks between the Twin Islands and Ashford Bay. I was embarrassed because at that moment the two older girls cruised by. In the late 1970s their example was my inspiration to buy my first sailboat in which to go single-handing.

The rigs on the *Wag* and the *Scotia* were similar. There were no gurdies as we know them today, with power to pull up heavy lead weights. The long cedar poles were mounted right alongside the mast,

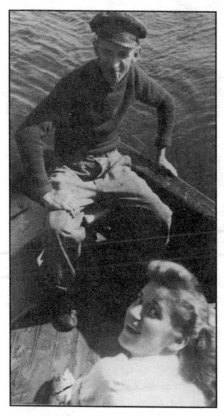

*June guts a salmon
while George Sr. steers.*

which was behind the cabin, as it is today. After we lowered these poles with the help of pulleys, we hooked the tag lines that were fastened to the poles to our fishing lines by means of a snap hook. The inside line, nearest to the hull, had three five-pound leads fastened in a row about two fathoms apart. The mainline was heavy, green, linen cod line, while the tailpiece that fastened to a swivel just at the top of the lead was a finer line called cutty hunk. Our actual leader, which we fastened to the lure where the fish's teeth might contact it, was made of about eighteen inches of fine brass piano wire coiled like a delicate spring. The outer line, at the outer end of the fishing pole, held only one lead weight and fished shallower, which was probably a good thing in the days before depth sounders. When the colour of the water changed, indicating a shoal, we could swing out and at least save our deep leads. When we had something on our lines we would hear a little bell ring on the trigger stick that was mounted on the pole where the leader line left it, much the same arrangement as today.

To protect their hands while they pulled in fifteen pounds of lead plus their quarry, some of the fishermen cut off sections of inner tube from Model T tires. These were skinny enough to just fit snugly around the hand with a hole cut in them for your thumb to stick through. But Dorothy said she relied on the tough wool of her Melton cloth jacket to protect her inner arm as she tucked it under the line in order to make a brake while she reached for another handhold on the line.

We could always hear the girls coming as their boat had a single-cylinder, five-horse Palmer engine that went *pong, pong, pong,* as it cruised along. To start it they had to spin the flywheel, and for electricity it had a dry-cell battery called a Hot-Shot. There was a coil and a governor to control the timing of the spark, which ignited the fuel in the cylinder. Dorothy's dad was always picking up fish nearby, so if anything went wrong they could easily get help. Still, one has to marvel at two eighteen-year-old girls managing to fish in a gas boat for the wily salmon. It was not an easy way to earn a wage, but certainly their earnings would outstrip the usual summer money earned by chambermaid work at resorts, especially when you add in the extra to be had from gathering dogfish livers. By the time autumn rolled around the girls would be richer both in money and self-esteem.

The good thing about the dogfishery was that it meant there were fewer of these sharks around for us salmon trollers to worry about. The bad thing that happened about that time was the appearance of what we called "Jap" weed. This new menace had arrived, along with the manila clams, when Japanese oyster spat was brought from Japan and adapted to the warm waters of Pendrell Sound. It took the oysters a while to adjust to our colder waters, but the fern-like weed that came along for the ride gleefully adapted to the new surroundings. Before many years had elapsed there was a dense forest of the brownish, feathery weed on every beach at about three feet below datum. In storms it broke loose and floated near the surface in pieces up to eight feet long. These were a total plague to trollers. Usually fishermen could see hazards like floating kelp and steer around them, but this weed lurked just below the surface, held up by the tiny bubble-like floats along its length. You couldn't miss it but you could certainly cuss it as you struggled to keep your lures clean. Over the years a fungus developed with an appetite for this newcomer, so eventually there were just straggly bits of it growing here and there, although it seems to be gradually increasing in some areas again. During the time that it flourished it caused us endless problems as well as severely diminished catches.

About this time my dad decided to fish for salmon with the *Loumar* so that he could get a better supply of gas. Pleasure cruising didn't rate as a wartime priority, but commercial fishing did. I gave up handtrolling and deckhanded for my family instead. Usually Dad pulled fish and I gutted. Although my presence was helpful, I no longer had the pride of self-earned money. Job stress coupled with a nasty bout of pleurisy-pneumonia had left my dad in frail health, so I felt I had no choice. We didn't exactly provide stiff competition for regular fishermen, but we did earn our gas allowance.

If wartime provided better income for fishermen, it also guaranteed a regular influx of young men into the area's logging industry. Logging was considered an essential industry, and if you were a conscientious objector you did well to get yourself into logging before you were called up by the draft.

One family that had logged the coast for years showed up around Cortez in 1941. Joe Martineau and his sons Bob, Frank, and Doug set to work logging Mary Island of the second growth and neglected trees that had been left by Marlatt. Joe prided himself on his selective logging practices, which are looked upon as a "new" invention these days.

The arrival of the Martineau clan brought much pleasure to the local dances, as the middle son was an amateur magician. He spent so much time perfecting his art that his brothers grumbled about having to do all the work at the camp. Martineau the Magician, as he called himself, kept us all mesmerized during a break in the dancing when Elmer Ellingsen, the accordionist, rested his fingers and his stomping right foot.

After the show a hat was passed around and the delighted audience threw in coins and dollars. At midnight the ladies served a supper consisting of sandwiches and cake that they had brought. Willing volunteers carried around huge jugs of tea or coffee, while others delivered canned milk and sugar, and stirring spoons were passed from hand to hand. Then we got back to the serious work of wearing out our shoe leather until the sun lit the way home.

If the dance was held at the Manson's hall we all walked the four miles there and back. When it was farther away we made the trip perched on the back of my Uncle Art's boat, the *Louise*, which we rechristened the "Lousy" because you got the full whiff of the exhaust that was piped out the side of the hull next to the engine. Uncle Art bought the boat from the government when all the Japanese fishermen were sent to internment camps and their boats were gathered together in a slough in the Fraser River and sold at bargain rates.

We'd start out on the *Louise* after supper of a Saturday evening and head for places like the Redonda Camp or the Gorge Harbour

Among the crew of volunteers that built the Gorge community hall in 1933 were Ed Tooker, George Beattie, Charlie Allen, Elsie Beattie, and Elsie's baby Margaret. (Margaret Schindler photo)

community hall, dance all night, then *put-put* home again to the song of the Easthope when dawn finally arrived. The whole Art Hayes family went with us and many other people arrived in the same fashion. The nearby dock was usually filled with boats.

The country dances featured everything from schottisches, heel and toe, polkas, and waltzes to well-called square dances. Only a handful of couples could dance the Swedish hambo, which became a showpiece. It was a delight to watch Helen and Peter Anderson of Turner Bay as they whirled through the intricate steps of this lovely dance. During the evening, each man made it his duty to see that every woman in the room was given a whirl, which made the party fun for just about everyone who came. The fact that you must accept an invitation to dance or else sit out that round was a trap in one way. There was a somewhat retarded fellow who was determined to find himself a wife. We'll call him Fritz for the sake of the story. When he looked your way you either hurried quickly out to the ladies cloakroom on the pretense of powdering your nose, refused the offer and sat out that dance, or, if you hadn't been quick enough to see him coming, you accepted his hand and were pushed slowly around the hall backwards, left, right, left, right, at the same pace no matter what the tune. You also had to put up with teasing. "Oh, I see you have a new boyfriend, June."

My dreadful cousin Rod tells of the Hallowe'en dance when he and his pals carefully picked up the girls outhouse at the school across the road and moved it about six feet back from its foundation. Then they hatched a plot with Fritz to go out and push it over. Making sure he was in the lead, they rushed out from the blinding gas lights, crossed the road, and ran down the path to the girls' facility, with the expected results.

As a city kid, I was grateful that the gym teacher at General Gordon School had taught us all the basic dance steps so that I didn't feel like too much of a dummy. The country kids had long since learned to dance when they tagged along to these social events as toddlers. No booze was served as there was no such thing as a liquor permit, but the drinkers made do with rounds out of a bottle outside.

With no TV, radio, or ferry off the island, the hall activities provided a real focus for the community. It also provided occasions for the men and the women to catch up on news and to renew old friendships.

WE GO SQUIRRELLY

One of my mother's favourite trips was a run to Squirrel Cove. If Dad had a machining problem that couldn't wait for Harry Dusenbury at Pender Harbour, we went around to see Harry Middleton in Squirrel Cove. His wife, Anna, was one of John Manson's daughters and had been a close friend of my mother long before Dad showed up on the island.

For a while before they were married, my parents had entertained ideas of pre-empting the property next to "Uncle" John's. Dad would have stayed on at the school and they would have farmed like everyone else. But the constraints on a teacher living among his employers were a major negative feature, and Dad was already well acquainted with them. The teacher was expected never to drink, swear, have political opinions, or behave in any non-approved manner. Leaving the island meant leaving old friends, but travelling to Squirrel Cove in the summer meant finding them again.

We children liked the Cove because of the stores. The postmaster, Laurie Forrest, had a small concession in the front of his house, but the large store was just down the beach, in the same building that holds the store now. Each of these establishments was different and each one gave you new choices about how to squander your few pennies.

In the early days, the big store had been run by George Ewart, who was almost as deaf as my mother. There was a boarding house in the back part of the building with the kitchen right in the rear. Sometimes a handlogger down on his luck would come into the shop and ask George as quietly as possible whether he could have a small loan, at which Mrs. Ewart would bellow from the back room, "We're not loaning any money today, George."

On a Sunday the place would be packed with loggers who had rowed or putted in from their small claims to stock up on the grub

The Loumar *hosts a back-deck picnic at Squirrel Cove.*
Raft-ups were fun. Alice Hayes looks on while
June watches the camera from Nora's lap.

that the steamship had delivered the night before. There would be
bulk produce—huge rounds of cheese, barrels of hardtack, and a
whole beef. George would ask you what cut of beef you wanted and
proceed to cut and saw the portion you required.

The steamship usually arrived between midnight and three in
the morning, and there could be as many as 25 people offloaded with
no place to go until daylight. No wonder Mrs. Ewart saw the need
for a boarding house. She and her Chinese cook, Ching, would feed
the lot come breakfast time. If the weather was too stormy for the
rowboats and small gas boats that came to pick them up, the facilities
really came into use. Irv Reedel, who later owned the store, said that
Ching was responsible for the huge garden and orchard, which
contained a wide variety of trees including apricots and peaches.
The canning boiler must have run full time in the autumn. There

were chickens, pigs, and a cow, so the place almost sustained itself in fresh supplies. When the third owner of the store, Blair Dickson, took over he brought Uncle Art's Caterpillar tractor over from Blind Creek and bulldozed out most of the orchard because he thought the trees were getting too old to bear crops. Likely a good pruning and tidying up would have been enough.

As if Mr. Ewart wasn't busy enough, he also sold fuel at the dock. At first it was in a large storage tank, but when salt water ate holes in the metal he resorted to drums. Using a hand pump he would pump fuel into a five-gallon container with a half-moon-shaped cover above the spout, then transfer this to a customer's gas tank by hand. Most boats carried their own generous funnel, usually with a felt shield over the screen to hold back as much water and rust as possible because, often as not, it rained the day you needed fuel. As well, the barrels were none too pristine. Perhaps it was as well that early boaters like my dad were handy with tools and that many of the early engines were not too fussy and accepted watery gas. If you needed coal oil for your lanterns and running lights, you bought it in a four-gallon square tin that had an arched metal handle on top and a little pouring spout with a screw-on cap. It cost fifteen cents a gallon.

Harry Middleton's house still stands just past the exit road from the store. It is a two-storey, shingle-covered building that sits right on the ground and has the usual tall, narrow, pioneer windows. Harry's machine shop, closer to the beach, was a big building with the usual forge and belt-driven machinery. Harry was a widely travelled man with knowledge about a lot of things. As a young man he had been working with a logging company at Gunflint Lake when the steam boiler blew up, killing his friend, the engineer. The shock put an end to Harry's logging career.

He was a machinist by trade and had learned his lathe work in Ontario. He also trained at the huge steam donkey plant in Sedro Wooley, Washington. When he heard that the Copper Mountain mine shop equipment, including a Cincinnati lathe and a four-cylinder Fairbanks engine, was available for a low price, he bought it and set up his business at Squirrel Cove. There was flat land near the beach for the house, machine shop, and marine ways, plus a school and a store for supplies for his family. (Copper Mountain, near Princeton, B.C., regularly went through cycles of boom or bust. Its various owners panicked each time the price of copper took a nose-dive, and many a B.C. machine shop enjoyed the bargains to be had during such a recession. Harry's Fairbanks engine is still being used in an old-style machine shop at Willow Point near Campbell River.)

Irv's son Fred Reedel, who grew up at Squirrel Cove, said that when he was a small boy he got a job turning the handle that pumped the bellows on Harry's forge. One of the job hazards was Harry's tendency to get distracted when someone came into the shop to have a job done. Part way through, Harry would stop working, start waving whatever tool he had in hand under the nose of his customer, and begin spouting about his latest "ism," which could be anything from communism to baptism. Fred said he'd go on steadily pumping to keep the coals hot because he never knew when the gust of talk would blow by, and Harry would expect the forge to be as it was when he began his tirade.

One day the talk did not let up until Harry said to his customer that it was lunchtime and asked him up to the house for a bite. By this time Fred's arm was just about falling off and his stomach was growling like a bear. As the men were leaving the shop, Mr. M. saw the boy and said, "Oh. Are you still here? You'd better go and get your lunch, too. We'll just bank up these coals and they'll be ready when we come back."

The creative skill of these early machinists is mindboggling today, when repair jobs mean ordering at the very least new parts, and at worst a whole new engine. Harry would take a one-cylinder Palmer that had a fixed head and remove everything above the base. He would machine a new cylinder—which he called a Middleton—using a special frame he had invented to hold it steady while he bored the inside, and then he would build a new piston. He also manufactured overhead valves, which he turned on his lathe, and could make the whole engine run again, provided nobody got him talking. If an engine needed new rings he simply cut and polished slices off an appropriate diameter of cast-iron pipe.

The fact that the Palmer and Easthope were cool-running, simple motors probably made innovation an easier task. The Easthope flywheel was supported by constant sleeve bearings that were composed of little rods that rolled in a housing. The Palmer flywheel had pillow blocks fore and aft with babbitt-lined bearings, which were fairly cheap to make and helped keep the price of the engine down. When these wore out, as they were bound to do, the mechanic simply bored out the old babbitt, heated a new batch on his forge, poured it into the mould, and rebored the opening. The curls of metal shone like pure silver as they peeled off the lathe, but by next day they were beginning to turn pewter dull. The Palmer was manufactured on the East Coast of the United States and was distributed exclusively in Western Canada by V.M. Dafoe, which still occupies the same premises on Powell Street in Vancouver. The 1948 price, which included everything from the engine to the propeller and electrical fittings, was listed at $456.92 for the little 5-8 horse motor, so it is easy to understand the Palmer's popularity.

When the job was done you'd ask, "How much?" and Harry would likely reply, "Oh, a couple of bucks." If you came into the shop and he showed little interest in your project, you just had to mention that so-and-so said the job couldn't be done and he would grab it from your hand, slap it on the bench, and get to work. And if you were foolish enough to argue with his latest philosophy, you were likely to get backed into a corner for a lecture with a red-hot poker wagging up and down in front of your face. The tirade always concluded with the question, "Do you get me, Steve?" even if your name was John.

One day Irv Reedel was in the shop, waiting for his job to be finished, when Alec Louis from the nearby Indian reserve came in, cradling the remains of the thrust bearing from his boat in his hands. He had a big cedar dugout with a four-horse gas engine for power. The bearing had collapsed and he'd lost most of the steel balls. Harry grabbed the handful, selected the two rings, dropped them into the forge to draw the temper out, put them on the lathe to recut the groove, then back in the forge to reheat and temper them. Then he reached down into a box of ball bearings, rustled around till he found some of the correct size, installed them, and handed the finished product to Alec. When he asked, "How much?" Harry replied, "Fifty cents."

Harry virtually lived in his shop. He would keep working until long after sundown. Irv remembered Harry grinding down a shaft, using his calipers now and then to test for size. It was so dark that Irv could hardly see the lathe when Harry stopped, removed the shaft, slapped on a little white lead paste, fitted it into the coupling, whacked it with a ten-pound hammer to drive it home, and said, "There, that'll do it."

In later years I talked to young Harry, then well into his sunset years. His father never let him into the shop. Often geniuses make

Tad Middleton, Nick Manson, Henry Pavid, and Ellen Middleton at Squirrel Cove in Nick's 1920 Ford car.

lousy teachers, as they have no patience with beginners. Apprenticing to someone like old Harry would have been impossible.

Through all this, Anna seemed to maintain her patience. Considering the minuscule amount her husband charged for the work and the number of times he invited people in for tea or whole meals while he talked the day away, one can only include his wife in the company of saints. That my mother loved her is no wonder, and if Anna complained about Harry to my mother, she kept it to herself. Apparently Anna's dad, John Manson, kept the household supplied with vegetables and meat from his farm, which allowed Harry to maintain his indifference to matters economic.

Beside Harry's shop and pull-out for boats at Squirrel Cove there was another marine ways run by a boatbuilder called Val (Valentine) Nichols. At one time Harry and Val had been partners, but a falling-out over politics drove them to set up separate businesses. In those days you were either fiercely Conservative or just as vehemently Liberal. Neither group had much time for the other (religious leanings were equally divisive).

The Nichols and their eleven children lived in a large house near the creek. Nora (Cowan) Thompson remembered having great fun visiting the Nichols' place as a child, with cocoa and toast always ready for the horde of youngsters to share. Mrs. N. had her husband build a wash house beside the creek to ease the laundry chore. In time this little building was home to a motor-driven washing machine like my grandmother's. Later Val had one of the first electric power plants on Cortez. He frugally put in just enough gas each night to last a few hours. This way he didn't have to go out in the dark to shut it down. His grandson, Fred Carr, said that when you heard the machine sputter you hurried to find the matches and lamp or, better yet, jumped right into bed. Fred also remembered that there was a telescope mounted on a tripod on the wide front veranda. He watched pods of blackfish (orcas) swim by up the Lewis Channel. Val used this device to keep track of local happenings.

Val produced fishing boats to order and also rebuilt those that were damaged or just suffered from old age. His plant took logs, cut the lumber, planed it to size, and produced the finished product. Watching a master builder fit a new plank is like seeing any skilled craftsman at work. The economy of movement, the confident use of tools, and the almost effortless appearance of the job make up a ballet. As a child I revelled in the sights, sounds, and smells of both of these places. Each shop used fire—the machinist to heat the metal and the boatbuilder to heat the water for the steam box he used for bending planks. But where the machine shop echoed with the ring of metal against metal, the shipbuilding sounds were gentler, often just the hiss of a plane or the thud of a wooden mallet driving home the fluffy cotton caulking that filled the seams between the planks.

Times were hard and frequently people did not pay their bills, so Val also built coffins for the Native settlement nearby. Every spring he and his son Charlie went up River's Inlet to gillnet, and sometimes there was work at Universal Timber Company in Redonda Bay. With so many kids to feed and clothe it took much creative scrabbling just to get by.

Harry and Val never exchanged a word, yet when Nichols needed some work done and sent his son over to Middleton, the job was done correctly and with alacrity, which was rather amazing since Harry was well known for taking a long time to get around to a job. When we were at Squirrel Cove to get something fixed, at least my dad could go down to the boat to wait if necessary.

As we motored back to Blind Creek we would pass the Smith homestead at Seaford. The big two-storey house was no longer home to Cap Smith, who had created this ranch out of nothing. When his wife left the children to his care so that she could live in the city, he hired a series of housekeepers to help raise his four daughters and one son. Housekeepers in those days got five dollars a month and board, along with all the responsibility of a parent. Cap Smith worked at nearby logging camps. Nellie (Smith) Jeffery remembered learning how to bake bread when she was ten, then rowing all the way into the Squirrel Cove Lagoon and hiking the trail to Von Donop Creek to carry it to her dad where he batched in his boat while working at a logging site.

Cap was loved by everyone who knew him except Ranson, the unstable recluse at Turn (Mary) Point, who had a habit of entrapping Smith's nanny goats should one be so foolish as to wander onto his property. As regularly as a goat went missing, Cap went and brought her home.

Katie (Smith) Thompson remembers being awakened one night by the sound of the kitchen door creaking open. She was sleeping in the downstairs bedroom with two of her sisters in the big double bed. Someone came quietly into their room and stood soundlessly at the foot of the bed, then turned and went up the stairs to her father's room. Cap Smith was away and his bed was empty, so the intruder returned and paused by the end of their bed again before leaving the house just as quietly. The frightened girls hurried to push every heavy piece of furniture they could move against the inside of the kitchen door before creeping back into bed to shiver. When their teenage brother returned from being with friends he raised hob to find the door blocked. I asked Katie who she thought had come into the house and she said it had to be Ranson because of the bulk of his outline against the dim light from the bedroom window. The children all had strict instructions never to visit his place.

One fateful day, after a southeast storm, Smith set out toward Turn Point in his rowboat, towing a skiff that he intended to fill with loose seaweed that the storm had ripped loose and washed up on the beaches. He used it to fertilize his garden. Cap Smith never returned. Next day the two boats were found washed up on the shore just north of Tiber Bay. The rowboat contained only a pair of gumboots and a drop of blood on the gunwale. Days of searching the ocean and beaches revealed no trace of this hardy pioneer. Without a body or firm evidence, the police could not follow up any leads to solve the mysterious disappearance of this skilled boatman.

I was never told of this tragedy when I was young, but I do remember my mother standing out on the back deck with her chin resting on her arms while she gazed at the homestead as we motored past on our way back from Squirrel Cove.

Partly because of his aloofness and inconsistent disposition, Ranson was credited with a number of incendiary incidents and was thought to be a person to be feared. However, he may have taken the blame for mischief that was actually the work of a dubious character who lived for a while on the Twin Islands and seemed bent on pointing the finger at the recluse. Whatever the reason for his bad reputation, Ranson's presence hardly enhanced local property values. My cousin Rod said he remembered seeing the tip of a shotgun come out of Ranson's cabin window as he rowed past. It followed the passerby carefully until he or she rounded the next point, then withdrew to await the return. Eventually this stopped. When no one had seen any sign of the recluse or his shotgun for about three weeks, Fraser Campbell finally got up the courage to knock on the door only to find it ajar and Ranson lying dead on the floor. He had been a fat man and the weather was unseasonably warm. The poor police had the unenviable job of bagging the body in the days before plastic. When curiosity finally outweighed fright young Rod and his friend Cal Campbell marvelled at the outline of the body formed by grease stains on the floorboards.

The next place we saw was Henry Tiber's, which was in the second to last little bay before you reached Turn Point. Henry, son of Augustus Tiber of Hague Lake, built himself a regular blacksmith's shop and did a lot of work both for the handloggers that populated the various inlets and for the oxen- and horse-powered logging shows nearby. Besides being a master blacksmith, Henry also built boats. He would choose a tree and ring the bark right down through the cambium layer and leave it standing for five years to season before he felled it to make a boat. The pioneers claim he was so inventive that he carved himself a usable set of false teeth from whalebone.

Henry and his wife had two daughters, Ethel and Myrtle Veronica. The photo of my dad with his Manson's class of 1921 shows Veronica, as she liked to be called, standing in the back row so she must have stayed with the grandparents during the school week. Veronica turned out to be a bit of a party girl. While still in her mid-teens she married Charlie, the youngest of the Byers brothers who lived near the Tiber home at Turn Point. Charlie was an outstanding boxer who could have fought professionally. He used to spar with his brothers after working all day in the woods. He also carried some of the emotional baggage that came from experiences in the awful war in Europe. The couple soon had a little girl called

Kathleen, but Veronica became disenchanted with marriage and longed for the bright lights of a metropolis. Onto the scene came a city slicker, Dara, who also happened to be a bit of a petty crook. Myrtle Veronica accepted his offer to take her to Vancouver and left with her daughter. When Charlie found out where they were, he set off to reclaim his wife. The resourceful Dara called for police protection from a "dangerous man who was out to kill him." When the police grabbed Charlie without explanation, he struck out with his fists, only to

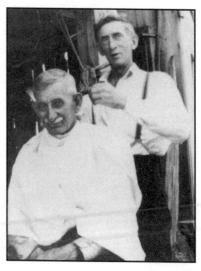

Henry Tiber getting his hair cut by Andy Byers. (Nellie Jeffery photo)

be beaten senseless with billy clubs. He returned to Cortez but never recovered from his injuries and later died in his orchard from a brain haemorrhage, with blood oozing from his ears and nose. My father claims he died of a broken heart, which is as good a way of putting it as any.

Dara eventually ended up in jail, so Veronica went on to Harrison where she found work cooking at young H.R. MacMillan's logging camp. In time she returned to Tiber Bay and thumbed her nose at convention by living her life as she pleased. Perhaps she was born 30 years too soon.

Another house that was near the Tibers' belonged to a Mr. Scofield, an Englishman who had spent time in the navy. He died in 1930 at the age of 68 after a prostate operation at the Powell River hospital. This calls into question the rumour that he was shot in his rowboat because he belonged to Jesse James' gang, although I'd be the first to admit the latter version is more intriguing.

Of course, as children we knew none of these stories. To us, Turn Point was synonymous with eagles. A nesting pair raised their young each year in a colossal old snag that stood in the little valley of the island at the turn where a giant arbutus tree now flourishes. We felt the parents to be most cruel to make their babies endure rain and sun on the raggedy platform of their exposed nest. One year Rod determined to capture a fledgling and raise it as a pet. He said that the tree was a horror to climb, smeared as it was in eagle droppings. Just as he was ready to peer over the edge of the nest, mama returned. He said he had no idea that he could descend a tree so rapidly. The tree no longer stands, although there is a new nesting tree on the next point toward Blind Creek.

If we were in the area of Turn Point and needed fuel, we could always go to Bliss Landing. The original developer of the store and wharf was a machinist by the name of Blistoe. From him came the name Blis' Landing. By the time we were going there, the Youngs had taken it over. They stored the fuel in large tanks and delivered it to boats through a hose, which meant less water and cleaner gas. Boyd Young had been at Port Simpson as the trader, first in a store right in the Native village and later at the site of the old Hudson's Bay Company fort. He spoke Chinook, the West Coast trading language. I suppose the long cold rainy winters and the slow demise of the fur trading industry drove the family south. In her excellent book *A Pour of Rain*, Boyd's daughter Helen Meilleur documents the Hudson's Bay Company involvement at Port Simpson and gives us a delightful account of her parents' experiences there with the Indian people.

Mr. Young was undoubtedly skilled at buying furs, but he had little experience with fish buying so got into hot water now and then with the local fishermen when he took over the buying job at Bliss Landing. There was a big difference between the price of red, pink, or white springs, just as there is now, and it takes a little practice to learn to spot the difference without actually cutting into the meat of the fish.

As well as fuel at the dock there was a small store in the building on shore. In the back of the building Mrs. Young had an aviary, as large as a small room, in which she raised canaries. Since the depopulation of the lower coast was getting into full swing, it seems likely that Bliss Landing was hardly a "get rich" operation.

Hallie Young seems to have been a woman of firm convictions. As a young teacher she bravely went to Alaska to teach school in a Tlingit village; she refused to fake a belief in religion or go to church with her husband and children at Port Simpson. In time she struck out on her own from the Bliss Landing store. With the family all grown and gone, her canaries obviously did not fill the void. One hopes she found an outlet for her good-humoured energy.

Bliss Landing, where Hallie Young kept an aviary in the store.
(Campbell River Museum photo)

Near Bliss Landing was Turner Bay, which was named for the first settler to live there. Robert James Turner was born on the Isle of Man in 1870. He was a veteran of both the Boer War and the British campaigns in India and had emigrated to Canada to find new adventures. My old chart numbered 3594, which is held together with love and Scotch tape, shows the name of Turner Bay in the wrong place. If you pass by the shore today you will still see the old foundation, the steep bluff to the left of it, and the new clearcut that stretches up the hill behind the house. Turner moved there with his family in the early 1910s, but sold out in 1924 when his wife left him. He put the house up for sale with all its furniture and 160 acres of land for $2000.

The lucky buyers were Helen and Peter Anderson, who had just returned from a stint of logging, first in Malaspina Inlet, then at Chancellor Channel, and finally at Port Neville. Helen said the house contained, among other things, a wind-up record player with tubular wax records as well as a fine sewing machine. Because they were so out of pocket by that time they sold these two items, but they did retain the large oak dining room suite with the many-leafed table and the matching sideboard with velvet lining in the drawers.

The farm was already well established with a goodly collection of fruit trees and berry bushes. Among the trees were many varieties of apples almost unknown to today's shopper. Aside from the usual king, transparent, pippin, Gravenstein, and russet apples there was one called a winter banana. The fruit was long and yellow in the fall, but if you left it on the tree all winter it turned a lovely orange colour with a red blush on one side. My friend Helen said that you could pick one of these apples in mid-winter and hardly be able to bite into it with the frost, but it still tasted great.

Helen's only child, Violet, was born shortly after she and Peter were married, just before they went to a handlogging claim on East Redonda Island. Years later I asked her how it was that she only had one child. She said that being the eldest and having had a lot

Helen, Violet, and Pete Anderson on board the Elephant *with its five h.p. Doman engine. (Helen Anderson photo)*

of work to do as a youngster with many smaller brothers and sisters, she vowed never to have a large family. When I marvelled at her success in keeping that vow, she said that the only preventative she knew about was the use of small chunks of cocoa butter. At that time it was still illegal in Canada to dispense either birth control information or supplies, but if Helen's method actually worked it could have saved many a pioneer woman from cracking under the strain. Some, like Cap Smith's wife, left when they could no longer stand the isolation, the constant pile of washing to be done the hard way, and the long rainy winters lived alone, totally responsible for the health and safety of an ever-increasing group of kids while their husbands worked away from the place, trying to earn enough money to make ends meet. To survive this challenge they needed to have either great neighbours or nearby relatives, or to have grown up in the environment. Helen managed to survive. She and Peter lived in Turner Bay until 1962.

When Pete was away fishing or logging to earn money to pay down the mortgage, Helen had a Fisherman's Co-op fish barge brought in and tied to their float. She not only milked the goats, baked the bread, caught fish for dinner, and chased bears out of her fruit trees, but she also managed the barge. She said it wasn't long before headquarters in Vancouver accused her of being short of weight in her shipments, especially in the cooked prawns. In those days of inadequate refrigeration, the two fishermen who caught prawns cooked them first before packing them into small wooden boxes that were then kept on ice. In desperation she nailed the boxes shut with a double row of small nails set in at angles to one another. When the packer arrived she overheard one guy say to the other, "Geeze, look what she's gone and done. Now we'll never get 'er open."

In some ways the fishermen themselves defeated their co-op. Because they had to wait until the end of the season to share in the profits, and because they only received partial payment for their catch when they offloaded, they often took the high-quality fish to the cash buyer. Helen says that she usually got just the scrap fish to handle.

Just to the south of Bliss Landing was Lund, a busy port with a store, hotel, and its related beer parlour. Lund was across from Savary Island, so it saw a lot of activity during the summer months, when the cottages were filled with people and the faithful Union boat bought the daddies up on Friday night and took them back to the city on Sunday.

Lund was also the home of Frank Osborne, who built the F.P. Osborne Heavy Duty marine engines in his shop. For those of us who think all useful engines have to be made in a huge factory, it comes as a surprise that one man in a humble machine shop could produce such a complicated device. Perhaps it also tells us what monopolies do to creativity and initiative. Osborne built both a one- and a two-cylinder engine, rated respectively at seven and fourteen horsepower. Any number of locally built boats were powered with his engines. Jim Spilsbury has an article about this amazing mechanic in *Raincoast Chronicles 11*.

Surprisingly enough, during the 1940s and 1950s there was a store on Sevilla Island, which almost blocks the entrance to Finn Bay, near Lund, providing good shelter from stormy seas at the dock. The storekeeper, Alec North, sold the usual supplies, with fuel available at his dock, and he ran a small shipyard nearby where he built boats. In retrospect it sounds like he had ten arms (and a helpful wife). He built a troller, the *Galley Bay*, for Ed Hanson (Helen Anderson's brother), which is still being fished. When it was built in 1946, to an Ed Monk design, it was thought to be foolishly large at 41 feet with an inside beam of a little over 12 feet. Alec installed the latest style of engine, a Chrysler Crown, rated at 110 horsepower. Yet in 1948 the warm Japanese current brought tuna in close to the Queen Charlotte Islands and Ed was able to go after them, fishing out as far as 60 miles offshore. That same year my brother George chartered the huge *Lady Royal* and fished tuna well off the coast at Ucluelet. Both Alec North and Ed were onto something of a trend, because the tiny shipyard went on to produce *Norlite*, *Wanderer #2*, *LorDel*, *Adolfina*, and *Finn Bay*. In the summer of 1993 I saw the *Adolfina* still fishing.

When we travelled on the *Loumar* during my childhood we usually limited our stop at Bliss Landing or Lund to the beginning of the trip back to Vancouver. The passage behind what we called the Ragged Islands, now known as the Copelands, was often clogged by several tugs hauling long, open booms to the mills in the city. They travelled so slowly that the deckhands had trolling poles propped up over the bulwarks. It was a time of great camaraderie on the seaway, as you always waved and passed the time of day with boats you met, which was an easy thing to do at eight knots or less of speed.

One summer we took Harry Daniels down to Savary Island opposite Lund to look at a horse that I believe belonged to Jim Spilsbury's mother. It was for sale because it was unmanageable. The horse, at some time during its life, had been turned into a barn where a bear was curled up in the manger. The bear made a decidedly un-Christian attack on the horse, leaving it scarred both physically and mentally. At any rate, on the return trip to Blind Creek we saw a huge whale breaching right out of the water, jumping over and over again, sending spray twenty feet high into the bright sunshine.

And, yes, Harry took the horse, and no, he didn't manage to make it any easier to handle. It shied and exploded into flailing hooves at the slightest provocation, giving me regular frights as I walked the path home to Blind Creek from my Aunt Mary's after dark.

OUR LOGGERS ARRIVE

In 1940 we arrived in Blind Creek from Vancouver to find our quiet bay completely changed. Uncle Art and Fraser Campbell had formed their own small company to clear our land of trees. They hired Nat Hodson as a faller, bought a used gas-driven donkey engine plus all the heavy gear needed, and set to work. It was an awful shock to see the devastation wrought on our grassy hillside.

The loggers had chosen a fine straight fir just back from the brow of the hill for a spar tree. After removing all the limbs and topping it, they fastened wire ropes on it until it looked like a giant water beetle stretching long legs out in all directions to get its balance. A huge bull block was rigged near the top, with a long mainline that ran out above the beach to be anchored securely to the big rock across the bay. As logs were cut, they were fastened by a cable called a choker to a haul-back cable, powered by the snorting donkey engine, that dragged them to the base of the spar tree.

When a big enough pile had accumulated, and when the tide was in, the logs were hoisted into the air, one or two at a time, and run down the mainline. As the end of the bundle hit the water, the choker came undone and the logs fell into the water with a resounding splash to bob about and wait for their companions within the pen. All of this activity was accompanied by much noise: the whistle punk's shrieked code to tell the donkey engineer what to do and to warn others to stand clear; the ripping, thumping progress of the chosen log as it was hoisted clear of the pile; the scream as it ran down to its fate in the water; the mighty splash of landing in the chuck; followed by a brief second of respectful silence before it all began again.

This job continued all summer and into the fall, at which time Uncle Art and Fraser managed to get a contract to clear the land to

Logging the Griffin site, where logs ran on a cable
past the house to splash down at high tide.

the east of the Daniels' place. To do this they had to buy a used Caterpillar tractor. The logs were tied close behind the tractor with their leading ends on a metal tray, which looked for all the world like a giant's dust pan. They were dragged out over mostly loamy soil and hauled down to the log dump at the creek where the trail used to start on its way up to the Daniels' at the top of the hill. The sad part about all this was that the little spawning stream was exposed to a lot of daylight and the tree cover that held the moisture on the upper hills was gone. Also our beach became muddy and smelly from dirt and loose bark brought down with the logs.

It took nature about twenty years to repair the damage to the beach and another twenty to re-cover most of the hillsides. As farming goes, raising trees requires the most patience. However, the loss of our trees provided the funds for Dad to add a kitchen onto the cottage and improve the bank balance in the bargain. Also, since a house and clearing were complete and the wintering by the Three Musketeers had met the residency requirements, the land was ours.

When the logging was going on and we were still building our summer place, I regularly went to spend time with my cousin Neen. It was often after dark in late August when it came time for me to go home. I was afraid to walk the path after dark because the Daniels' horse was let out to forage and he would neigh and gallop off with a thunder of hooves that set my heart to pounding. My Aunt Mary would have to take an empty tobacco can, punch a hole on one side, and bend the corners inward to make a holder into which she would push a candle. (A deluxe model of this illumination, called a "bug," had a wire hoop handle and holes punched in the bottom to prevent blow-outs.) When it was ready I held the candle by its lower end and lit it, producing a bright ray of light not unlike a cheap flashlight. The odd hot drip of wax ran down onto my hand, but it was worth the pain to have the comfort of being able to see the path or the eyes of a deer before it surprised me by bounding away. If I was not watchful and didn't keep pushing the candle up through its snug hole, it would burn down, drop out, and really leave me in the dark. At any rate, a goodly supply of matches gave me confidence. As I gradually collected a pile of "bugs" I had to remember to return them or else hurry away before dark, because my aunt would run out of building materials.

One night, just after the logging Cat had been through the path, my brother and I started out for home without a bug because he was far too brave for such nonsense. As we neared the swampy area, a low spot in the trail near where the Royal Vancouver Yacht Club now has its driveway, our hair rose stiffly on end. Eerie, fluorescent green lights were glowing up from the path right in front of us. George finally got the courage to kick at them and they turned out to be chunks of rotted wood that had been churned to the surface by the Cat tracks.

Years later, on this same path, my mother and her little cocker spaniel were returning after dark from taking bread up to her parents' place. The dog barked up ahead and Mother stopped just in time to avoid tripping over the still-oozing carcass of a deer. A cougar was undoubtedly in the bush nearby, waiting for the intruders to get along so he could enjoy his dinner. It was probably a good thing he'd found the deer before he noticed the small dog.

In 1940 there was still lots of work to do on the property. Dad built a temporary float that was tied beside steep Red Granite Bluff. We pulled ourselves back and forth to shore in a dinghy and started tidying up the hillside and clearing space among the stumps to fence the garden. There was enough straight-grain cedar left in broken trees that hadn't been worth removing for us to cut eight-foot pickets for our fence. Grandpa Hayes came down to help, so the chips and dirt flew.

Since one Grandpa was worth two of me, I got to walk up and keep my dearly loved Grandma company. We usually communicated by my writing questions or answers, as her deafness was almost total by now. Sometimes I went out to play with the young goats, or I laboriously ground wheat in a hand grinder for the chickens to eat. It was cheaper to buy the whole grain and it kept longer, but the chickens more readily digested cracked wheat. The poultry lived in a pen on the hillside behind the house. There was a huge old yew tree that stood with its toes in the chicken yard to provide shade for the hens and chewy berries for me. It was not until years later that I learned these berries are classed as poisonous. Certainly the hens and I enjoyed their reddish-orange meat that tasted much like jujubes.

Marjorie and George splitting pickets for the garden fence at Blind Creek.

I had my work cut out if I intended to make any sort of a meal of them, as they had large pointed pits that filled their centres and peeked out from the ends.

I would also fetch water for Grandma. Once when I was down by the well with the two buckets and the yoke used to carry them I saw the bees from one of Grandpa's hives begin to swarm. He always kept at least two hives active for the honey and for the pollinating done by these buzzing workers. The twirling cloud landed way up in a fir tree above Great-Uncle Arthur's old cabin. Usually when this happened Grandpa simply put on his beekeeper's hat and veil, lit up his smoker to stun them, gathered up the bees, and put them in a new home, but this was one group that never had to share the sweet harvest again. It was well out of reach of his ladder.

It was not until I set out to write this book that I found to my surprise that my grandmother did know how to cook. Certainly I had never seen her by the stove, as she always seemed to be in bed with a migraine or heart pains. Whenever we visited for a meal my mother had done the work. None of my cousins were aware that Grandma was celebrated for her ability to take an old laying hen and turn it into a mouth-watering roasted chicken. Aunt Alice remembers venison with cranberry jelly, or roast beef and Yorkshire pudding when Grandpa returned home from Powell River with an apple box full of groceries, and there were suet puddings that would cause today's doctors to shake their heads at the cholesterol hazard involved. Alice also told me that when Grandma was in her teens, she had been apprenticed to a woman caterer, Mrs. Ingram, in Winnipeg who specialized in meals for visiting royalty, so this would explain the skill in the kitchen. I do recall the little cloth bags of goat cheese hung out to cure on the line, but since my tastes were undeveloped at that age, I did not realize what a gourmet delight this represented.

I also learned from my friend Nellie, who had gone to school at Seaford with my aunts, that the Hayes' sandwiches were always made with delicious, crunchy brown bread containing wheat that had been ground in the same grinder I used to feed the hens. Grandma soaked the cracked wheat overnight and added it to the white flour along with water from the potatoes cooked the night before. All the kids with white sandwiches gleefully traded with my aunts, who were only too happy to eat different food.

At my grandparents' house there were many toys and books to entertain us, including *Boy's Own Annuals* that had oodles of stories about life in English boarding schools. Hare-and-hounds chases and how-to-do-its filled the pages of these large, thick treasures. There were also steamer trunks with remnants of Grandma's finery. Seven daughters had long since modified the modifiable, but there were still bits and pieces to try on. I found my grandmother's handmade, eyelet ruffled pantaloons. These were tied behind at the waist with a drawstring and cunningly split from the mid-belly right under the crotch to the back waistband. Now I understood how pioneer women with all those long skirts and petticoats could relieve themselves along the wagon trails west! Come to think of it, a quick roll in the hay would have been a lot easier in those days before pantyhose was invented, or looking at it another way, a woman was a lot more vulnerable under all her coverings than she is now. I later learned that a Mrs. Bloomer in England invented the first closed crotch

George made it to the back row before his carefully balanced camera took a dive. His goal was to capture himself with all the Hayes' descendants in 1933. In the back row are Marjorie, George, Nerine, Art, Bill Illman, Dorothy, Alice, Jack (behind), Florence, Nora, Bettie. In the front, Georgie, Alf with young Nerine, Mary with baby Frank, Florence with June, and Roddie, amid Alf's flowers.

underwear for women, and it took her idea a while to catch on. A true unthinking teenager, I quickly cut away all the between-the-legs part of those beautifully hand-stitched pantaloons and resewed them to produce a currently fashionable crinoline, never realizing the sacrilege I was committing.

When I tired of inside activities, there was always the orchard with its golden grasses and windfall apples. Years later, when I attended a workshop for teachers at the Hotel Vancouver, we were asked to close our eyes and envision a place where we were completely at peace and happy. It took only seconds before I could smell and feel the prickly scythed grass beneath my shoulders, see the wisps of summer clouds through leafy tree branches, and taste the sharp juiciness of Grandpa's Gravenstein apples as I bit into their tart, sun-warmed goodness in his precious orchard that had brought him such pleasure and so much disappointment. The sense of peace that pervaded my soul when I experienced this vision is almost beyond description. We were told to hang on to this state until we could see someone coming toward us to bring us a message. Gradually a misty form emerged, telling me to use the gifts God had given me to paint and to write. Since at that time in my life I was in the midst of grieving for the loss of both my brother and my marriage, and my encroaching deafness was filling me with fear, this revelation was most gratefully received. Whenever I feel overwhelmed I return in my mind to Grandpa's orchard.

Outside the Hayes' gate in the direction of the beach there were two little cottages that stood just within my Great-Uncle Arthur Ashford's property. They were empty by this time. Bundle Inn no longer held Rod and Bettie, and my violin-playing Great-Uncle Arthur had died and was buried in the little cemetery at the west end of Bartholomew Road. He was a shy, quiet, deaf gentleman who became mired in the money-losing orchard game like my grandpa. When he first arrived at Cortez he built a fine log cabin between the goat barn and the sea. I think at that time he would have had a view out toward the Twin Islands. One night a fierce southeast storm blew a big maple tree down across the house where Great-Uncle Arthur slept. The roof was crushed but the sturdy log walls kept the weight of the tree trunk from crashing right down to the floor. Many island people came to marvel at the sight and at his close brush with death.

My cousin Roddy and my brother found some boxes of old steel-jacketed .303 rifle shells in the wreckage. They quietly sneaked some cartons away and hid them in bracken among some windfalls. When they figured everybody had forgotten about the adventure, they lit a beach fire and threw shells into it to hear the most satisfying explosions. Since hunting out of season was not an uncommon occurrence, they got away with it on several occasions. However, that fall Grandpa decided to get rid of the dead bracken and lit a brush fire, with the inevitable result. The neighbours must have thought war had broken out unbeknownst to them because the resulting volleys echoed off the bluffs and went on until all the shells were consumed. Rod said that George got off lightly because he was by now safely in Vancouver; it was the younger cousin who got the licking. Certainly the two little boys had no idea how closely they had flirted with death, although the spanking probably left its own impression on Rod.

After the loss of his house my great-uncle moved into one of the cabins built for the Hayes girls when they were teenagers. He lived out the rest of his lonely life in the one-roomed, shake-covered, pioneer dwelling that was fairly typical of hand-built shelters of the time. There was not a drop of paint on the bare cedar, but it looked natural, sitting where the goats could browse around it. The shack was different from most in that there was no real cooking equipment. Great-Uncle Arthur took his meals at the bigger house—a logical arrangement seeing that he was providing all the goat products to the household. Years later, when I went into the little cabin I could still feel the warmth of Arthur's presence. I think memories like this spring from aroma as much as anything.

A typical one-room shack. This one at the Anderson place had one door in the front with a single window beside it. (Helen Anderson photo)

Maybe the aroma was partly goat, but if so, it was not unpleasant. The nannies and the baby goats had a warm, sun-drenched animal smell, but the billy goat's stench was a throat-choking, urine-drenched gasper. He was beautiful with his long, silky, yellowed white fur blowing in the breeze, but he was only beautiful when you were upwind. I never saw the billy goat around the barn, so he wasn't hard to avoid.

The advantage of keeping goats was their ability to forage without the need for much pasture. The fact that they had access to any outdoor food they chose sometimes flavoured the milk, but it certainly improved the taste of the meat. This is a noticeable feature of most island-raised meat, especially lamb: the huckleberry shines through. Unlike cows, the goats seemed to enjoy coming home in the evening. Of course, there was always an edible treat for them,

Alf Hayes and Cougar Smith with his cougar hounds.

but I think they just enjoyed the human contact. When the luxury of oranges appeared in the house, Great-Uncle Arthur dried the peelings on top of the stove warming shelf. The goats would follow along behind him, gently butting at him to share the treat.

For wintertime, Grandpa cut hay by hand with a scythe all around his fruit trees and in the bottom land between the orchard and the house. He moved it with the Ford truck to the shake-covered goat barn on Great-Uncle Arthur's property. The goats spent time lazing around in this building in the worst of the winter weather and also when the baby goats were young, especially if there was a cougar in the area. Otherwise they roamed freely on the hillsides nearby.

Whenever the *Loumar* came around into Ashford Bay the goats would talk to us from the bluffs. They appeared to hold on with the help of a dab of glue. Because they grazed on anything they could reach, the undergrowth was kept in control and the small shoots of alder were stripped bare. Alder is as much a plague to a stump rancher as dandelions are to a greens keeper. In the first spring of their life you can simply pull them out by hand, but if you miss this opportunity you lose any bare ground you had carefully cleared the year before.

George Sr. rows the cousins to Loumar *after a beach picnic.*

To the west of Ashford Bay was the Jeffery place. Apparently Mr. J. had developed tuberculosis after being gassed in World War I. With antibiotics still a distant dream, the only treatment available at that time was a diet that emphasized fresh fruits and vegetables, bed rest, fresh air, and sunbathing. That was the regime practised at the provincial sanatorium at Tranquille, near Kamloops, where he had gone until the disease cleared up. Although the gassing and subsequent TB was a terrible price to pay for being patriotic, it did leave Mr. Jeffery with a small pension. The more I look at it, the more I realize outside money was one of the necessities for survival on the island, whether that money came from logging earnings, remittances from home, or government pensions.

The Jefferys came to Cortez in 1925 on the advice of a friend when their house in North Vancouver was destroyed by fire. Mr. Jeffery bought the Butler place between Blind Creek and Turn Point, which was glowingly described as the ideal place to raise a family. The Jefferys landed at Seaford with no one to meet them and started walking with their few possessions, including infant daughter Betty and the other five youngsters, in the general direction of their property. The road petered out just beyond the school, so they returned to Seaford where they had seen a house. Soon Cap Smith had them loaded on his gas boat, the *Seagull*, and took them around to Butler's homestead.

When Mrs. Jeffery, a city dweller, got a good look at their stump ranch home, she staged a rebellion. During the war in Europe, while her husband was cooking near the front for the army, Mrs. Jeffery

Captain Marion Enos Smith and his son Francis on the Seagull, *the boat he used for handlogging, c. 1924. (Nellie Jeffery photo)*

had returned to England, left her two young boys with relatives, and found a job as matron of a hostel for young women who were working for the military. This experience had left her as someone to be reckoned with; when she said "Jump," you jumped. As a result, they soon relocated to a rental place near Squirrel Cove while Mr. Jeffery looked for better accommodation. Before too long he found the place next to Grandpa Hayes', and once he added on to the large single room he had a usable house for his family. Although it was no closer to a store, it was on a decent road with neighbours nearby, so Mrs. Jeffery could entertain at tea and catch a hair-raising ride with my grandpa to church at Manson's Landing.

When the Padgett place and most of the Smelt Bay waterfront came up for sale in the mid-1930s, Grandpa Jeff was astute enough to buy it so that his children and their families could settle in this choice location. (The provincial government later bought the site of the old Native village from Jeffery relatives to establish a park and campsite that are enjoyed by many visitors to the island.)

Logging in the days before steel hardhats were required claimed the life of Charlie, the second oldest Jeffery boy. He was struck on the head by what was called a widow-maker as he was falling a tree and died as they passed the Ragged Islands while being rushed by gas boat from Ramsay Arm to Powell River. Freddie, the youngest son, lasted through most of World War II but was killed during the last days of the Italian campaign. A daughter, Lillian, was married to

Mr. and Mrs. Jeffery with their daughter Betty and their granddaughters, Judy and Joan (Baron and Nellie's children), at the Jeffery homestead, Chris' Lagoon, c. 1940. (Nellie Jeffery photo)

Jack Parry and spent much of her life at Refuge Cove. That indiscriminate killer, cancer, took both her life and that of her brother Baron while they were in their prime. The two remaining sisters still live at Smelt Bay, as does my very dear friend Nellie Jeffery, the widow of Baron, happily surrounded by children, grandchildren, great-grandchildren, and the incredible collection of Indian artifacts that she has found over the years since she was born at Seaford.

If you travel by boat today past where the Jefferys used to live, you will see the large, bare, rocky islet that sat in front of the house. You will not see the salt lagoon, then known as Chris' Lagoon, as it has become completely landlocked, with gravel piled up at the entrance by the tumbling winter surf.

This whole area has lost much of its earlier beauty. Although the Japanese logged it at the turn of the century, their activity was repaired by nature by the time I arrived. Upstream from the shady, cliff-edged lagoon was a clear little creek that flowed out of my Uncle

*A common wartime scene on Cortez was the gathering of locals near
the Manson's Landing post office (in background) when the Union
Steamship approached with its cargo of groceries, mail, and freight.
Walter Beasley is on the left, next to Nellie Jeffery. Her daughters Judy
and Joan are in front, and her father-in-law is in the background on the
left. Others in the scene include Postmaster Patterson, far right, and
Ernie Bartholomew next to him. (Nellie Jeffery photo)*

Bill Illman's pasture. Today the paved road passes by a waterlogged
pool, filled with ugly dead trees, that local people swear has always
been like that. They did not wade the length of that pretty waterway
looking for the delicate sand and wood-chip tubes of the caddis fly
larvae that lay so well disguised on the shadow and sunlight dappled
stream bed. The clear running water coursed gently until it passed
through a wooden culvert under the two dirt tracks in the shady
road and joined the waters of the lagoon. Dog salmon came up this
creek to spawn. Dolly (Jeffery) Hansen remembers catching them in
the fall so that they could be smoked for winter use.

The return of the beaver, which had been hunted to near
extinction during Hudson's Bay trading days, coupled with sloppy
road construction put an end to the little creek that had provided a
nursery for baby salmon.

World War II brought changes to another part of the island. Just
past the top of the Twin (Ulloa) Islands there was the Jap ranch. Mr.
Nakasui, the man who had title to the property, was said to have

At Clay's wharf in 1944, brother George works on his fishing boat, Wag, *while June watches from the back deck of the* Loumar. *Sometimes the* Wag's *old engine gave up and George caught a tow from the* Loumar *(below).*

been an officer in the Imperial Navy before he and his wife came in 1915 to settle on what had been the headquarters for a huge Japanese ox-logging outfit at the turn of the century. When Grandpa caught an octopus instead of a cod he would paddle it along to the Nakasuis. They were absolutely delighted to pay two dollars for the catch.

As neighbours they were courteous and well-liked, but after Pearl Harbour and the alleged sightings of submarines off the B.C. coast, even before the declaration of war, the locals became understandably nervous. The Nakasuis were evacuated to internment camps along with all Japanese people living on the coast, and the fruit from their orchard was left to rot. When we went by in the fall to pick some apples to take back to the city with us, we found their home stripped of belongings. Unwanted objects littered the ground. It made me ashamed to be Canadian.

I had never been to that farm before and was impressed with the neatness and beauty of the surroundings. The outhouse especially interested us children because it was a communal affair, with two long smooth poles, one at the back of your knees and the other at the rear to keep you from falling in, along which people could sit side by side. As children from a Victorian background, we had not been aware that such lack of prudishness existed in the world.

We also envied them their obvious craving for beautiful surroundings. Everything was aesthetically pleasing as well as tidy and purposeful. There was a lovely grape arbour that was loaded with plump cones of grapes ready for winemaking. The well-pruned fruit trees from which we gathered winter apples are still being cultivated today, but not by the original farmers.

The machine logging of areas like our pre-emption, which had been picked over at an earlier time, also signalled change: the end of handlogging as we had known it. We no longer saw the small camps that had still existed up passageways in Desolation Sound when we first cruised on the *Loumar*. And it was not just the loggers who were leaving or amalgamating with others; more and more homesteads were deserted, leaving burdened fruit trees for orchardless people like ourselves to visit for our winter supply of apples. At least three boxes made the trip back to town each year, tied under canvas on the top deck of the boat to be snugged away in our sawdust-insulated basement storeroom.

WAR'S AFTERMATH

Since we had no radio, we heard about the war's end from the neighbours at Cortez. After the euphoria evaporated, changes began. A group of ex-navy fellows bought a steel-hulled Fairmile corvette that had been built by Star Shipyard in New Westminster in 1944 for wartime use, converted this sleek boat to freight and passenger use, and initiated a fast service upcoast to the Desolation Sound area. They got a government float and wharf shed built in Blind Creek and came swooshing into the bay bringing freight and passengers. The *Gulf Wing* was both lean and fast (compared to other boats of the days), with a cruising speed of 12.5 knots and a maximum of 15. The operators often overnighted on the boat at Blind Creek, bending elbows happily with the local loggers and heading out next day for the fast run to Vancouver.

You could board the boat in Vancouver at 9:30 in the morning, be at Westview by 3:30, and at any one of several stops at Cortez in time for dinner. The *Gulf Stream*, a former navy patrol boat, was outfitted to carry up to 225 passengers. By 1946, to more effectively serve the freighting business, a Bangor class vessel was brought in from back east and renamed the *Gulf Mariner*.

The vigorous competition was soon felt by the old Union Steamship Company, which still travelled its slow, tedious route. Perhaps the company became too complacent through the years with the government mail-carrying contracts, and possibly the shareholders were also unwilling to take risks given that shipping rates had been frozen in wartime, making the profit margin narrow. Whatever the reason, after the disastrous accident involving one of the Gulf Lines boats at Dinner Rock we bitterly regretted the steamships' decline. The accident claimed the lives of five people, including Henry Pavid's infant daughter, Jeannie.

Gulf Stream *leaving Blind Creek with Griffin float*
and Loumar *in mid-distance.*

According to a report in a special edition of the *Powell River News* dated Sunday, October 12, 1947, the *Gulf Stream* hit the rock while going full speed just after dark. The vessel ran up the steep angle of the shore for about one third of its length, then tipped sharply to port, trapping those who had already gone to their staterooms aft. More lives would have been lost had it not been for heroic efforts on the part of crew members such as Captain Frank Peterson. Peterson smashed open the salon window with his bare hands and hauled out Mrs. Walkem, widow of the late president of the Gulf of Georgia Towing Company. Norman Hope of Refuge Cove was also credited with saving a number of lives. The force of the crash snatched Henry Pavid's daughter from his hands. He was unable to find her in the dark swirling waters before he, too, struggled out of the opening. The resulting court hearing eventually closed down this fledgling company, effectively hastening the isolation of Desolation Sound ports.

After our corner of Blind Creek was restored to us and cleared of booms, my Uncle Art's end of Blind Creek turned into a log dump. He had been joined by the Hansen Brothers, Ken and Harold, who brought their families and floathouses and pulled them up on the beach near the Hayes' place. Fraser Campbell and his family were already there, making it a small village. They logged back of Art's place and gradually worked their way in the direction of Irv MacKay's ranch. The logging took many years. It produced the road that now gets you to the Squirrel Cove connection from the head of Blind Creek. This narrow logging road snaked down alongside a bluff and made an abrupt turn at the bottom to take you on two big logs across the old creek bed before you ground your way back up another hill.

Logging was exhausting work for Uncle Art because he was a small-framed man, but he kept at it, trying to match pace with the younger men. The outcome of all this sweat was an upturn in their fortunes. Eventually Mary got the house of her dreams, furnished the way she wanted it, but her family had grown and were gone almost before the paint had dried. This left my aunt and uncle to rattle around by themselves in the two-storey, four-bedroom, yellow house that still stands at the head of the bay. Eventually they sold everything, built a fish boat (the *Debbie Marie*), banked the balance, and went commercial salmon fishing with friends in the Blackfish Sound area.

Around this time Uncle Dick had a bigger troller built, the *Euridyce*, which almost turned turtle when launched. Like his first boat, this one was top-heavy. Once enough ballast was added, he set off to fish around Spider Island and beyond, eventually making Prince Rupert his main port for replenishing liquid supplies. Aunt Bettie stayed at home for a few seasons but soon realized that if she was going to keep her husband alive she'd better learn to fish with him.

Both my fishing aunts wrote newsy letters to my mother in the city about their life afloat. I wish now that I had saved all of Mary's, as they would have made a wonderful book. They frequently went in to Minstrel Island for supplies and for what she called a "harbour day," when she did the laundry, baked bread, wrote letters, and visited with the few fishermen's wives who were there while Art restored gear and talked with his buddies. In later years I asked her about those years on the boat. To my surprise she said she was bored nearly to tears by the fishing because Art wouldn't let her pull lines. He was afraid she'd wreck his expensive gurdies. Pulling in fish is where the fun is, but she had to sit at the wheel hour after hour, trying to stay awake while she dodged driftwood and other trollers. No wonder fishermen and their deckhands smoked to help pass the time away. Lung cancer took its toll on Mary as well as many other fisher folk.

The end of World War II was also when the Hope brothers with their wives bought Refuge Cove from Jack Tindall. The brothers,

Refuge Cove store in the mid-1940s. (Maryann McCoy photo)

Buster (Douglas) with his wife Vivian, and Norman with his gregarious wife Doris, brought a lot of humour, industry, and business acumen to this little outpost. Both Norman and Doris came into storekeeping with zest, leaving behind jobs that ill-fitted their abilities and dispositions.

As a teenager, Norman had accepted the role of family provider so that several of his equally brilliant brothers could remain in school. By the time the opportunity at Refuge Cove came along he was plugging away at a dull job in a plumbing store.

Doris, from her English public school background where Latin shared equal billing with etiquette, had, for reasons of economy, sadly given up her ambition to become a teacher. She accepted a scholarship to business college, which she won as a member of Vancouver's Dawson School choir that had just been awarded top marks in the provincial choir competition. Trained in stenography but unable to get work, she finally found a job as a telephone operator, a role totally unsuited to an extrovert as watchful supervisors enforced restrictions that prevented any interaction between operators, their clients, or their working partners while at the switchboard. The resulting stress kept Doris well supplied with migraine headaches. When she got married her job was terminated as single women had priority in the workplace. It is easy to see how someone like Doris would thrive in the varied roles provided by country storekeeping.

Refuge Cove had always been famous for its dance evenings, when all the display cases were pushed back against the wall and

Sunday was "boat day" at Refuge Cove, a time to shop and visit. Here handloggers Bill Wood and Frank Armitage, who worked at Walsh Cove, stand near their old Walronda.*(Maryann McCoy photo)*

people arrived by boat to twirl the night away. The Hopes installed a speaker system so the square dance caller could be heard over the chatter of voices and the clatter of feet. One unforgettable Christmas the Union Steamship boat brought in food and 73 passengers to add to the already lively crowd of locals. Doris said that the floors had been so damaged by loggers coming in during the week in their caulk boots that she had to vacuum up the sawdust before they could shove the counters back into position the next day.

Running a store as a partnership is never an easy task so in 1950, when a nearby logging outfit with a large debt to the store sold its camp to the Hopes as partial payment, Norman and Doris decided to try their hand at managing a logging show. Doris swept through the untidy camp like an avenging angel, washing board-stiff blankets that had never met soap; adding ends to the six-foot-long denim sheets so they could be tucked in; emptying pillows to wash the grimy ticking; and climbing up on a kitchen chair balanced on top of a table to spray Vello, the water-based paint of the time, on the blackened walls and ceilings. She used her Electrolux vacuum spray attachment to propel the paint, with some ending up on the floor and some on herself. She even painted over the pitted floors and left firm instructions about how the bunkhouse was to be kept in future. If the fellows provided the kindling and wood, she'd light their fire so they could dry out after a wet day in the woods. If the kindling wasn't ready they were out of luck.

It became a happy, productive camp that provided work for many local people like Ed Tooker, his brother Frank, and Nellie Jeffery, who put in a stint as cook while her husband, Baron, drove a truck. By 1958 Buster and Vivian were ready to move to the city so that their daughter could have better access to schooling, so Norm and Doris returned to Refuge Cove and the business they loved best. Because you can't run a country store from a separate house, they modified the accommodation at the back of the store, putting in adequate heating and a new dining area that overlooked the water. A rattan and bamboo motif that covered a multitude of structural oddities turned it into livable space. In 1972 the business was bought out by the co-operative that continues to own and operate the store as well as the surrounding land and housing. The store is now a seasonal business instead of enjoying the year-round hum of activity known to the early pioneers. If it weren't for the handful of dedicated co-op owners, the place would stagnate and die, as have so many coastal centres.

In 1998 Doris Hope was still living in her home at Refuge Cove, where she has a good view of all the activity during the hectic summer months. Although she was the first local person to own and run an outboard motor, she has had to give up going out alone in her little skiff in which she joyously fished for all those years. She enjoys a steady stream of company during the summer, and her intelligence and humour keep the conversation lively. These days I travel regularly to the Cove for fuel, water, and a visit to Doris so that I can return to Blind Creek tanked up with both supplies and a new stock of jokes to share.

Things changed around Blind Creek as well. My brother sold the *Wag* and spent a season or two deckhanding at Ucluelet with Aunt Nora's fisherman husband, Bill Wesnedge. Then he went to the University of B.C., intent on becoming a fisheries officer. After spending a summer indoors at Nanaimo Research Station, he made the decision to be a commercial fisherman and remain his own boss. He left university after the first year and happily pursued his dream. I missed him and spent my sixteenth summer muttering about all my friends in the city learning to play tennis and here was I just fishing or learning how to handle a boat. My dad stopped my unreasonable whining by stating that this was likely the last summer they had to enjoy my company and why didn't I just relax and enjoy it, too?

That fall, when it was time to return home, the relentless surge of southeast storms that had begun in mid-August just kept on rolling in. Dad was vice-principal at Moberly Elementary School and had to be there, so one morning he departed on the *Gulf Wing*, leaving Mother and me to return to Vancouver with the *Loumar* when the weather moderated. I had a boyfriend at the time, Pete McMartin, who was a deckhand on the tug *La Riene* during his summer break from university. He volunteered to get as far north as Lund by riding his thumb so that he could help us on the trip, so Mother and I pulled up the two huge navy anchors that had held *Loumar* in our bay and set out for Lund. We were supremely happy to be handling the boat by ourselves and I wish, in retrospect, that we had made the whole trip alone. It would have done so much for our feelings of self-worth.

When Pete gunned the engines the next day as though he were running a tug, Mother shook her head but said nothing. We rolled up a mighty tug bow-wave and impressive wake and were almost out of fuel by the time we arrived at Pope's Landing in Pender Harbour, where Nerine and Ned Garvey had made their home. Mother bought more gas and said that in future we would run like a sedate cruiser because she did not have the resources of a tugboat skipper nor the desire to burn out bearings on the way home. In Pender Harbour we tied up alongside the *Esmerelda*, a graceful, double-ended cruiser belonging to friends. Mother had an enjoyable visit without my dad dominating the conversation. Usually her deafness left her sitting holding her cigarette with a smile painted on her lips as she tried to look like she was joining in with whatever was being discussed. To say that I was happy to be holding hands again would be an understatement. I had missed my handsome skiing buddy.

That was my last year on the *Loumar*. The next summer I gathered three friends and we went to work at Goose Bay for the Canadian Fish Company. I went off to the University of B.C. in the fall with enough earnings to pay for my books, clothing, and much of my tuition. Next spring my dad was still not well, something that becomes obvious when you see pictures of him taken at that time, looking like a walking skeleton. The doctor said he felt early retirement was a good idea. In those days that meant a pension of $48 per month, which was about one-third of a beginning teacher's salary. He hung on another year while I went regretfully to Normal School. I was afraid to face life alone so married another student teacher and closed a chapter of my life. I was not to finish my schooling nor return to Cortez until the 1970s.

By summer the house was sold. The *Loumar* was also sold to a returned navy man because my parents needed the money. He listened with superior disdain while Dad told him about what bearings to grease and how often it was to be done. On the trip north he ran the bearings dry, drove the boat up onto some remote beach, and took Dad to court. All the money had to be refunded and the sturdy companion of my youth was abandoned. So far as I know, it was never refloated. How I wish I had had the courage to accept the job the city offered me, take out a mortgage on the *Loumar*, and live aboard at Clay's wharf. I longed for the sea and bitterly regretted leaving it.

I know we can't go back, no matter how much we wish to do so. When Grandmother Hayes died I went to the little cottage where she had lived out her last years near Mary and Art's house, secure in the knowledge that at least I could get her collection of dairies and write her life story. The diaries were gone. When I asked about them, Mary said that Bettie had burned them all because she thought they were private. All that I found was the old wicker basket filled with dolls that had been sent out to Winnipeg at the turn of the century for Grandma's many daughters to enjoy. I hugged the dolls and cried.

EPILOGUE

U p until now I had never really viewed my grandfather's life as being what is known as a *success*. There never seemed to be extra money for small luxuries, meals came off the farm, and clothes were patched. Certainly the arrival of the Old Age Pension, as it was known in those days, was greeted with a sigh of relief. Yet Grandpa always seemed content as he went about his tasks humming or whistling.

Like most couples, my grandparents' goals in life were probably different. It appeared that Alf never wanted anything more than to be able to care for his own holdings, nurture his creations, and live within the seasons. That my grandmother's dreams were not his dreams never seemed to sway his devotion to the task.

He must have gained great pleasure from his correspondence with Luther Burbank. He saved all of Luther's letters along with his own diaries in which he recorded in minute print all the records of the weather, his activities in relation to the farm, and his successes and failures. Whether he was gathering up his swarming bees, scything hay in the orchard, or mending picket fences against the marauding deer, he always seemed to be smiling. Although he may not have been able to provide my grandmother with the manor house of her dreams, he was no doubt a success in the eyes of Mr. Burbank, whose carefully tended acreage in Santa Rosa has become a tourist attraction. Success for my grandfather was not found in amassing great wealth but in discovering that his roses and plums had survived yet another winter.

I returned to the Hayes farm in the summer of 1997 with some anxiety because previous visits had brought nothing but disappointment. The series of non-agricultural owners had not appeared to value the great knowledge and care that Alf had invested in the place. Also, the blackberries were gradually smothering everything. To my great delight the new owners, Bill and Elena Wheeler were restoring the property to its old splendour.

On a chance trip in the late 1970s, accompanying a friend who was part of a group bidding on what was to become Linnea Farm, Bill had a look at listings in the area. He was completely mesmerized by the atmosphere at the old Hayes place, which was also up for sale. It was merged with another property, and the size of the merged block put the cost far above his budget. Yet Bill, who grew up in the farming area of Vermont, knew this was where he wanted to live and work. He kept in touch with the local real estate agent, and when the speculators finally decided to divide the property into smaller holdings, she let him know that Grandpa and Great-Uncle Arthur's orchards were included in one of the parcels.

That Bill should have eventually been led to this warm green bowl carved out of the forest on Cortez Island is nothing short of karma. The pity is that it hadn't happened years earlier when the roses and plums were still safe from the eager teeth of the deer.

The first owners after my grandparents found the metal trunk full of Alf's carefully preserved letters and diaries. It had been hauled outside by local acquisitors who found it contained nothing they valued. The winter rains had done their damage, so the new owners burned the lot. They also cut down and burned the huge sugar maple tree that stood by the edge of the path near the root house and yielded maple sugar if conditions were right. (The root house, which was placed so the winter sun could find it but the winds couldn't, was a little room dug into a hillside with thick log walls and a good roof. It was lined with shelves for apples and bins for unwashed potatoes, carrots, and turnips; the latter two were packed in sand to protect them from drying out.)

Now Bill and Elena are faced with the task of determining if the prolific walnut trees near the gate grew from Luther Burbank stock. It may be that Alf Hayes' letters written to Luther in the 1920s are preserved among the Burbank correspondence that is safely locked away in the U.S. Department of Agriculture Library in Maryland. If so, it would be a great help.

An offspring of the sweet golden plum named for my grandmother lay nearly dead in Great-Uncle Arthur's orchard. It was down on its side stripped of all growth save for three branches that reached begging arms to the sky. Bill and Elena were able to graft cuttings from these onto sturdy root stock and currently list it in their catalogue as Hayes Plum 3. They have formed a small company called Inner Coast Nursery and are selling young trees propagated from the Hayes stock as well as other finds from among the island's gardens. Much care has gone into identifying all the old apples, pears, plums, peaches, cherries, medlars, and quince as well as the nut trees. This farm is now one of a number of small holdings working to preserve diversity in orchards.

Of all the roses that flourished down the rockeries in front of the house, only a few survived. There is a pink climber over the gate to the nursery garden that looks like one my mother used to have over a trellis in Blind Creek. If so, it is one of Alf's creations. The magenta "Florence Ashford" climber spreads its perfume into the airs of Smelt Bay where it arches over the entrance to Betty Jeffery's vegetable garden. Maybe Elena will take a cutting back to its birthplace.

And, wonder of wonders, I heard a gentle baa-ing as I roamed among the trees, but no, it wasn't a goat. The Wheelers keep a flock of sheep to mow the grass under the trees as well as to control the blackberries and broom that threatened to take over the fields. Muscovy Ducks do their share of gobbling up insects that would also do some damage. Bill has to work at another job to help support their dream while Elena works hard on the property, but maybe, just maybe, the electronic world we live in today will help to spread the word about what this little gem of a farm has to offer.

REFERENCES

Anderson, Doris. *Evergreen Islands*. Sidney, BC: Gray's Publishing Ltd., 1979.

Blanchet, M. Wylie. *The Curve of Time*. Sidney, BC: Gray's Publishing Ltd., 1968.

Burkinshaw, Robert K. *False Creek* (Occasional Paper No.2). Vancouver: City of Vancouver Archives, 1984.

Garner, Joe. *Never Chop Your Rope*. Nanaimo, BC: Cinnibar Press Ltd., 1988.

Haig-Brown, Alan. "Galley Bay" in *The Westcoast Fisherman*, August 1989.

Hill, Beth. *Upcoast Summers*. Ganges, BC: Horsdal and Schubart Publishers Ltd., 1985.

Lambert, Gertie. "Cortez Island Back Then" in *Raincoast Chronicles 11 Up*. Madeira Park, BC: Harbour Publishing Co. Ltd., 1994.

Lambert, John. *My Diary for 1909*. The original is in the possession of his grandson, Stuart Lambert, of the Powell River area. A copy exists at the Powell River Museum.

May, Robin. *The Gold Rushes*. New York: Hippocrene Books, 1978.

Meilleur, Helen. *A Pour of Rain*. Victoria: Sono Nis Press, 1980.

Patterson, T.W. *The Empress of Canada: A Century of Adventure*. Victoria: The Daily Colonist, 1971.

Peterson, Lester R. *The Story of the Sechelt Nation*. Madeira Park, BC: Harbour Publishing Co. Ltd., 1990.

Pethick, Derek. *Vancouver Recalled*. Surrey, BC: Hancock House Publishers, 1974.

Pinkerton, Kathrene. *Three's a Crew.* Ganges, BC: Horsdal and Schubart Publishers Ltd., 1991.

Powell River's First 50 Years. Powell River, BC: A.H. Asgard, Publisher, 1960.

Powell River Digester. Powell River Museum. Company publication in booklet form. 1921-1928.

Rushton, Gerald. *Echoes of the Whistle.* Vancouver: Douglas and McIntyre, 1980.

———. *Whistle up the Inlet.* Vancouver: Douglas and McIntyre, 1974.

Smith, Frank. *Writing and the Writer.* New York: Holt Rinehart and Winston, 1982.

Spilsbury, Jim. "They Don't Make 'Em Anymore Dept.: Frank Osborne" in *Raincoast Chronicles 11 Up.* Madeira Park, BC: Harbour Publishing Co. Ltd., 1994.

Thompson, Bill. *Once Upon a Stump.* Powell River, BC: Powell River Heritage Association, 1993.

Tuchman, Barbara W. *The Proud Tower. A Portrait of the World Before the War: 1890-1914.* New York: Macmillan Publishing, 1962.

Whitlock, Ralph. *A Victorian Village.* London: Robert Hale Limited, 1990.

Wolferstan, Bill. *Pacific Yachting's Cruising Guide to BC Volume II: Desolation Sound.* Toronto: Maclean-Hunter, 1980.

INDEX

Index

Index

THE AUTHOR

Spending her childhood along the B.C. coast helped prepare writer/artist June Cameron to become the first woman to race her own boat in all the major B.C. sailing races. She went on to cruise the B.C. shoreline, often alone, sending articles regularly to be published in Pacific Yachting magazine, as well as painting many boat portraits.

In order to research this book she moved onto a small diesel-powered cruiser to seek out the pioneers who generously contributed both their memories and photographs to enhance this history.

June holds a masters degree from the University of British Columbia in special needs communication.